TEACHING AND WRITING
Case studies

A practical guide

John Heath

EUROPEAN CASE CLEARING HOUSE

D1340171

Published in 1998 by The European Case Clearing House
Cranfield University, Wharley End
Bedford MK43 0JR England
Tel: +44 (0)1234 750903
Fax: +44 (0)1234 751125
E-mail: ECCH@cranfield.ac.uk
Web site: http://www.ecch.cranfield.ac.uk

ISBN 0 907815 01 4

Printed in UK
Production editor: Helen Riddiough

The author

John Heath is an independent management consultant. He has been a
tutor on case development workshops throughout the world since
1974. A regular contributor of cases
to the European Case Clearing
House (ECCH), he served as a member of its Executive Committee for
15 years.

He has an MBA from Cranfield School of Management
and taught strategic management on the Leicester
Business School MBA programme, which he directed for
five years.

He has written cases for the Open University Business
School and the UK Ministry of Defence, and has lectured
on case teaching at the International Teachers'
Programme, INSEAD.

Contents

ix   PREFACE

xi   INTRODUCTION

PART ONE   TEACHING WITH CASE STUDIES

3   Section 1.1   Learning and teaching

11   Section 1.2   The case method

13   Section 1.3   Learning through cases

17   Section 1.4   Guiding a case discussion

21   Section 1.5   Discussing the Holmesafe case

35   Section 1.6   Using case incidents

41   Section 1.7   Role playing

45   Section 1.8   Preparing students to learn through cases

49   Section 1.9   Developing your case teaching skills

55   Section 1.10 Using case studies in examinations

     PART TWO   WRITING CASE STUDIES

61   Section 2.1   Case development

63   Section 2.2   Field research

69   Section 2.3   Desk-based and armchair cases

73   Section 2.4   Writing the case draft

81   Section 2.5   Case structure

93   Section 2.6   Editing the case draft

101 Section 2.7   The case teaching note

105 Section 2.8   Case release

     EXERCISES

113 Using news items

115 A question of authority

117   Mallards Department Store

121   Hall Nurseries

125   Case drafting: Geoff Brown

131   Case drafting: Meadows Machinery plc

APPENDICES

137   Case research preparation

141   Cases on small businesses: Writer's brief

145   Getting it right: Malcolm Bradbury

149   Holmesafe Ltd: Teaching note

159   Tasks of the case teacher

161   Cases in management: A student's guide

165   Case incidents: A student's guide

169   REFERENCES AND SOURCES

173   INDEX

Preface

The aim of this guide is to help new or relatively inexperienced users and writers of case studies to get to grips with this highly effective vehicle for learning. Part One explores the use of cases in teaching and Part Two looks at the task of writing teaching cases.

Introduced to the case method as an MBA student 25 years ago I was immediately 'hooked', and have been teaching, writing and talking about cases ever since.

The guide contains a combination of what I have learned from fellow case teachers and writers around the world and what I have discovered for myself. With the passage of time the distinction between the two has sometimes become a little blurred. Consequently, I am uncertain as to the origin of some of the ideas presented here. So, if an acknowledgement has been overlooked I offer my sincere apologies.

In any event, my thanks are due to countless friends and colleagues whose thoughts on the case teaching process are echoed in this guide. But they are due especially to my wife Pat, for her support and patience during my long preoccupation with this most rewarding of learning vehicles.

John Heath
Wells
October 1997

Introduction

A case study is a vehicle for learning. It can be briefly defined as:

> *An account or description of a situation, or sequence of events, which raises issues or problems for analysis and solution.*

For the purposes of this guide I have adopted a rather loose definition and have regarded as a case study any description or account of events that can be used to foster learning. The terms 'case' and 'case study' will be used interchangeably in this guide although some writers draw a distinction between them.

Cases are now widely used in many areas of education and training. The focus of this guide, however, is mainly on their use in business and management education and training. We shall consider the use of cases at both under-graduate and post-graduate level and also look at their role in supervisor and manager development pro-grammes.

The 'case method' is associated, in particular, with the Harvard Business School, where the analysis and discussion of cases is the predominant mode of learning, and case development is a major focus of research effort. Cases were introduced into Harvard's business administration courses in the early 1900s and the first book of written cases appeared in 1921. Cases were already widely used in the study of medicine and law. Their introduction within the new faculty of business administration was rooted in the belief that here, as in medicine and law, Harvard was in the business of training practitioners.

The education and training of doctors, lawyers and managers alike requires the development of both knowledge and skills. Not only must they know things – they must also be able to act effectively in their respective professions. To this end, the study of cases taken from the real world in which trainees are soon to practise makes an effective and enduring contribution.

Cases come in a variety of forms and are used in a number of different ways, as we shall see. But a case is only one element within a case learning system. If that system is to be effective we must also consider the other elements within the system. This we will do as we consider how to use cases to bring about learning, and how to write cases that facilitate this process.

Part One

TEACHING WITH
Case studies

Learning and teaching

If we are to explore the business of learning and teaching with cases, perhaps we should start by saying a little about the nature of learning and teaching.

Learning can be simply defined as the acquisition of knowledge, skills and attitudes.

So if at the end of a case teaching session students know something they did not know before, or can do something they could not do before (or do it better), or have formed a view about something that they did not have before, then they have learned.

So what is teaching? It can be summed up as the process of bringing about learning. On this basis a teacher may be regarded as a designer and manager of learning events or situations.

In designing a learning session we need to consider a number of elements.

- Who is to do the learning (and teaching)?
- What is to be learned?
- How is it to be learned?
- Where, and under what conditions, is it to be learned?

3

Who is to do the learning?

We need to start any learning session from where the students are. What are they bringing to the session in terms of existing knowledge, skills and attitudes? It is upon this existing base that we have to build.

What is to be learned?

To keep things simple it is assumed that the desired learning outcome – what is to be learned – is specified by some external authority – examination board, professional body or employer. However, I recognise that in some instances what is to be learned may be subject to negotiation with the learner. Students may question *why* something is to be learned. Further exploration of this issue may be outside the scope of this guide, but we must recognise as teachers that desired learning objectives can only be achieved if the learner is ready, able and *willing* to learn.

How is it to be learned?

A useful model of the learning process is that shown in the box below.

The Lancaster model identifies three modes of learning – knowledge input, discovery and reflection.

Knowledge input involves the acquisition of data, factual information and concepts. In an educational setting knowledge is acquired formally through structured activities, including reading, lectures and lessons of various kinds. It also takes place in a less structured manner through the countless everyday interactions that occur between a person's senses and the environment.

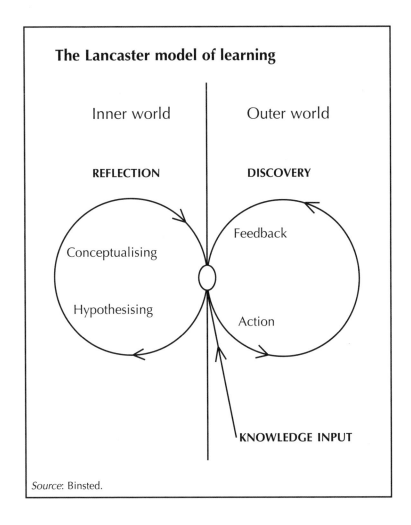

The Lancaster model of learning

Inner world | Outer world

REFLECTION | DISCOVERY

Feedback

Conceptualising

Hypothesising

Action

KNOWLEDGE INPUT

Source: Binsted.

Discovery is essentially a two-stage process in which the learner acts and notes the consequences of that action. It is an action–feedback process. If the results of the action are satisfactory then positive feedback is generated. This signals to the learner that the action was appropriate to the situation. In similar future circumstances the event will be recalled and the successful behaviour repeated. If it is again successful further positive feedback reinforces the learning. If the situation in question is a frequent occurrence, the behaviour may become habitual, triggered subconsciously by the situational 'environment'.

If the initial action produces unsatisfactory results the negative feedback received indicates that the action was inappropriate in the situation and needs to be modified. The feedback triggered by the learner's actions may be self-generated or provided by others.

Reflection involves restructuring experiences and observations in the mind, making sense of them, conceptualising and generating theories or hypotheses about what has happened. In this way the learner constantly restructures his or her view of the world in the light of new experiences and information.

These three modes of learning may be regarded as components of a learning cycle, some of which occur entirely within the mind of the learner and others in the outer world with which the learner interacts. The modes may be identified in any learning event either on their own or in combination.

The Lancaster model provides a useful framework against which the case teacher and case writer may consider a number of issues. We need to ask ourselves such questions as: how can I design a whole loop cycle which maximises learning opportunities? Should I seek to take the student through all three modes or only one or two? In what sequence should the learning event progress through the modes and with what frequency?

Different sequences can achieve different objectives. Two examples illustrate this:

> *Input – Discovery – Reflection*
>
> Here is some data and a procedure. Apply the procedure to the data and come back with some conclusions.

> *Discovery – Reflection – Input*
>
> Experience this activity. Then come together and we'll discuss what is happening and why. Then I'll tell you what researchers have found out about it.

A merit of the Lancaster model is that it confronts us with a range of challenging alternatives that help to develop our ability to design effective learning events.

Case teaching and the Lancaster model

Most case teachers believe that case teaching is not a particularly effective way of imparting knowledge (although it is true that a good deal of vicarious knowledge is acquired through reading cases). They see the contribution of case teaching to be principally in the areas of skills and attitude development. This development takes place through the actions of the learner and their resulting feedback.

Reflecting upon these ongoing experiences leads to continual adjustment in the learner's understanding of the world. The discussion of a case study provides many opportunities for such reflection and it is part of the case teacher's job to encourage actively this mode of learning.

Structure and feedback

Among the variables affecting a teacher's choice of learning method is the degree of structure it imposes on the session and the feedback available to learners during the session. The straight lecture, for example, has a traditional inflexible structure in which a passive audience is talked at by the lecturer. There is normally no other interaction between lecturer and audience. The communication is in one direction only and consequently there is no feedback available to the learner.

An unscripted role play, by contrast, has no predetermined pattern. It will develop in ways that depend on the evolving actions and responses of those involved. There is a continuous cycle of action and feedback as the session proceeds.

Teaching methods with varying degrees of structure and feedback are shown below.

Forms of learning session

	High			
			Role play, Game	
Feedback		Programmed learning	Discussion of a case study	Tutorial
			Lesson	
	Low	High	*Imposed structure*	Low

Source: Simmons (1974).

Case teaching may be regarded as positioned mid-way along each dimension, with opportunities for some adjustment along both axes. What this means in practical terms we shall explore later.

Where, and under what conditions, is it to be learned?

The existing knowledge, experience and number of learners who are to take part must be taken into account in designing a learning event. The facilities available and the environment in which learning is to take place are also important. Some environments are more conducive to learning than others. Thus, the environment in which a session is to take place will influence the design of that event, either by offering new opportunities or by imposing specific constraints.

Of particular significance in shaping a session will be the teacher's beliefs about how people learn. We each have our own views about this, based partly on theory and partly on our experience as teachers. My own experiences have tended to confirm the points listed in the box below.

Beliefs about how people learn

We only learn what we are interested in learning

Learning depends on wanting to learn

We learn best when we are free to create our own responses in a situation

Learning depends on not knowing the answers

Learning is largely an emotional experience

The above comments on teaching and learning will, I hope, give the reader some insight into the foundations upon which I approach case teaching and case writing. It should also provide a helpful backdrop against which to consider the remainder of this guide.

The case method

In this guide the term case method is used to mean any use of cases for teaching and learning. This may offend some purists, for whom the case method has a more restricted meaning. They might define it along the following lines:

> *Student discussion of a planned sequence of cases drawn from actual situations with responsibility for analysis and conclusions about issues within the case resting with the students. The focus is on students learning through their own joint efforts. The case teacher's role is seen as one of guiding student discussion rather than providing answers.*

My own experience of the classic case method, as an MBA student in the early 1970s, involved an ongoing diet of three cases a day. We read and analysed the cases individually each evening, together with relevant sections of course texts. Next, the cases were discussed first in small study groups, and finally in a plenary session of the whole class led by the case teacher. Most courses on the programme were taught entirely by this method.

Although I found this intensive, virtually exclusive use of cases to be very effective, this view was not shared by all course members. People have different preferences and reactions to learning approaches and it seems to me important to reflect this by using a variety of methods in our teaching. So while the use of cases is promoted in this guide, it is recognised that the case is only one tool in the teacher's tool kit, to be used when it appears to offer the best prospect for bringing about the desired learning. The test of a particular teaching method should be, 'Does it work'?

Case studies have proved effective in developing the following skills

Analysis and critical thinking

Decision making

Judging between different courses of action

Handling assumptions and inferences

Presenting a point of view

Listening to and understanding others

Relating theory to practice

Learning through cases

Cases come in many different forms and are used in a variety of ways. Different types of case are shown below. Among these, the situation case comes most readily to mind when case studies are mentioned. The case examples discussed in this guide are mainly of this type. We shall also look at the use of case incidents, since these can be a useful means of introducing students to learning through cases.

Types of case study

The incident case

This is a very short case that describes a single incident. It can be used during a lecture or lesson to illustrate a concept or to raise an issue for discussion. It can be read quickly and normally needs no pre-class preparation by students. Case incidents can be a useful way of introducing students to the case method.

The background case

The main purpose is merely to impart information in a way that has greater interest than a conventional reading or handout. Students identify more readily with data presented in case form than they would with an impersonal document. A typical background case can be used as a framework within which other cases explore specific issues.

The exercise case

This provides an opportunity for the student to apply a specific technique and is widely used where quantitative analysis is required. The manipulation of numerical data within the context of a real situation is more interesting for the student than the use of the same skills as a purely academic exercise.

The situation case

This is the type usually envisaged when the term 'case study' is mentioned. The student is asked to make an analysis of the information embodied in the case and to delineate the significant relationships existing among the various items of data. This often involves the question 'why did things go wrong and how could this have been avoided?'.

The complex case

This is a development of the situation type where the significant issues are immersed in a mass of data, much of which is irrelevant. The problem for the student is to distinguish the vital issues from a number of superficial ones which serve only to distract the attention. A further complication is that the embodied issues may be interdependent.

The decision case

This goes a step further than those listed above. Here the student is required to state what he or she would do in the circumstances described and to formulate an action plan. In order to do this the student must develop a variety of feasible approaches and then exercise judgement in selecting that which appears to have the highest probability of success.

Given the wide range of learning objectives and individual preferences in learning and teaching styles, it is clear that case studies can be used in many different ways. A common approach is for the case study to be considered first by individual course members and then discussed within a small group. This is usually followed by a plenary session of all course members led by the course tutor.

Ways of using case studies

Students prepare an individual written analysis

Small groups discuss the case study, with or without set questions

A student, or group of students, presents a recommended course of action to the class and its merits are debated

The teacher leads a discussion drawing out desired learning points. Key points may be summarised by the teacher at the end of the session to consolidate learning

For most case teachers the plenary discussion is at the heart of the case method. It is here that good case teachers come into their own. For them, case teaching is about guiding a process of discovery. Its effectiveness depends upon *well-crafted questions* posed to students, *sensitive listening* and *constructive responses*. It is on this aspect of case teaching that we shall focus in the next section.

Guiding a case discussion

Most case studies raise more than one issue for discussion and the tutor may guide course members to particular issues by careful choice of questions, especially those with which he or she opens the discussion. The questions chosen will, of course, be influenced by the learning objectives being pursued. Listed below are some sample questions and the orientation they may be used to achieve.

What is the problem here?
- Problem identification

How do you feel about...?
What is your view of the behaviour described?
- Attitude/opinion eliciting

What do you notice about...?
- Attention drawing

What other examples are there of...?
- Thought provoking
- Generalising from the specific

How do you think X felt in this situation?
- Sensitivity to others' feelings
- Empathy generation

What might be done to...?
- Problem solving/reducing

What else might be done?
- Generation of alternatives

Would you do that?
- Personal preferences

What would be the cost of doing that?
- Proposal evaluation (Note: *'cost'* in *all* its forms)

What would you do in this situation?
- Identification with/ownership of the situation discussed

What do you feel about Y's (a course member) suggestion/assessment/attitude?
- Group interaction/sharing

Can you develop Z's (a course member) idea a little more?
- Team building

The list is by no means exhaustive, and tutors will no doubt wish to experiment. It can be useful, on occasions, for the tutor to ask deliberately provocative questions. These can reveal differences of opinion or indicate the possibility of a much wider interpretation of an issue than the group had previously considered.

The analyses, comments and opinions of participants should be probed by the tutors to ensure that issues are explored at an appropriate depth. The interaction should not be predominantly between tutor and course members. The tutor should develop interaction among course members themselves. They should be encouraged to give adequate consideration to the views of their course colleagues and to maintain an open mind during the discussion. Where views differ they should be invited to ask themselves why it is that their course colleagues view things differently.

Having listened to a variety of views, and given careful consideration to them, group members should be encouraged to decide their own position on the particular issue and be prepared to defend it.

Through questions, restatements and summary remarks at critical points during the discussion, the effective tutor will ensure that a vigorous exchange takes place and that the issues raised by the case study under consideration are properly examined. Under his or her guidance course members will move towards a deeper understanding of the issues identified within the case.

Group processes

The learning objectives for a session may include the parallel development of interpersonal skills and specific subject knowledge. If so, the tutor may invite group members, from time to time, to consider the processes at work within the discussion group. What do members think makes for an effective group discussion? Are these characteristics and behaviours indicative of team effectiveness generally? Among the behaviours which group members might be encouraged to identify, or on which their observations can be invited, are those listed below.

Contributing to group effectiveness

Initiating and contributing ideas and information

Giving and asking for information, ideas, opinions and feelings

Clarifying, synthesising and giving examples

Periodically summarising what has taken place and the major points discussed

Encouraging and supporting participation by all members

Evaluating the effectiveness of the group and diagnosing difficulties in group functioning

Process observing

Giving direction to the discussion

Energising the discussion

Helping the sending and receiving skills of members

Being an active listener

Testing whether decisions have been made and what the procedure has been

Moderating controversies by disagreeing with others in ways that promote intellectual disagreement without personal rejection (and helping other members to disagree in the same way)

Discussing the Holmesafe case

Now that some general points have been made on leading case discussions these will now be applied to a particular case, Holmesafe Ltd.

The students with whom this case is used are at the beginning of a course on business strategy and already have some basic knowledge of marketing and finance. They may be undergraduates on a business studies course or more mature students studying for a management diploma.

They have been asked to read the case before the session and to consider the issues it raises. Other than that, they have been given no specific assignment concerning the case. Importantly though, they have been briefed on the case method and its role among the range of learning methods available, and have accepted the demands it places upon both learner and teacher if it is to be fully effective.

The class normally comprises 20 to 30 students sitting at desks arranged in a horseshoe pattern facing a large white board. With this arrangement students are able to see and communicate with the tutor and one another. There is an overhead projector and a large flip-chart at each side of the white board. There is room for the tutor to move around within the horseshoe during the discussion. (It is recognised that many tutors are less fortunate in terms of their teaching accommodation and class sizes.)

Now the scene has been set for the discussion you may find it helpful to read the case and undertake your own analysis of it.

HOLMESAFE LTD

Three years ago George Holmes, an engineer, hit upon an idea for a novel security device and produced a successful prototype in his workshop. He made some enquiries through friends to try to find a buyer and was introduced to Frank Jackson, a buyer for the wholesale company of Dawsons Ltd.

Jackson offered to discuss the marketing of the product with his immediate superior, Harry Thomas, who was the chief buyer with Dawsons. A meeting was arranged between the three men at which Holmes had a chance to form an opinion of the characters of Jackson and Thomas. He judged that Thomas was a somewhat distant man of high integrity who was prepared to leave action to his more vigorous subordinate Jackson, whose influence with Thomas appeared to be considerable. On the other hand, Holmes felt that Jackson was warm, unscrupulous where the interests of his company, and possibly himself, were concerned, and very active in furthering a cause in which he was interested.

A trial batch of the devices was made for Dawsons and these were easily sold. Further quantities were made and sold in the same way and by the end of the first three months it became clear that the demand for the product was going to increase. There was also an increase in demand for an advisory service on the installation of the new device and more generally on the problems of electronic security. With the demand on his time increasing, Holmes recruited first one friend, and then two more and between them they were able to manage the business on a part-time basis for the first year. Holmes spent some time cultivating Jackson, and generally being as friendly and affable as circumstances permitted. In turn, Jackson assisted Holmes by pushing sales of the new product and, just as important, ensured that Dawsons paid all bills promptly.

The first year's 'trading' produced good results and the four friends celebrated with a theatre and supper party to which Jackson and his wife were invited, and they made a present of a case of whisky to Jackson. Sales continued to increase and the four decided to form a company, Holmesafe Ltd, with themselves as directors. They asked Jackson to become the fifth director. When he mentioned this to Thomas the latter pointed out that as Jackson would be purchasing goods for Dawsons from Holmesafe this would involve a conflict of interests for him. Jackson recognised the force of this argument and with expressions of regret he turned down the invitation to become a director of Holmesafe.

During their first year of operation as a limited company it became clear that the market had been underestimated. Dawsons' demands were greater than anticipated and a large retail chain also took a substantial volume of goods. Sales to smaller companies also became appreciable and fees from the advisory service also increased. The company could no longer manage on a part-time basis and an old school friend of Holmes became the company's first full-time employee. Halfway through the year a contract was signed with a large national building contractor for Holmesafe to provide an advisory service on home security. Later in the year the company moved into new rented premises and took on a full-time secretary. Income and expenditure for Holmesafe's first year of operations are shown in Table 1.

Table 2 shows the company's projected income and expenditure for the second year of operation.

About mid-way through the second year Holmes received a phone call from Jackson which, after the usual greetings, proceeded as follows:

Jackson: *I thought I'd better let you know that I'm coming under increasing pressure to buy security devices from Browns. They are very similar in performance to yours. Browns have improved their manufacturing methods and are now extremely competitive and very reliable.*

Holmes: *But surely our reputation is worth a great deal. You have put a lot of effort into this yourself and it would be a pity if it were all wasted.*

Jackson: *Sure, and I'll obviously do what I can. But I thought I should let you know how the land lies. Incidentally, there is a bit of personal advice I'd like from you. You remember I used to play in a band a few evenings a week? Well, for personal reasons I have had to give that up and it has left me a bit short of cash. So I'm looking for an evening job that will bring me in a few pounds a week. Got any ideas?*

Holmes: *I don't know of anything offhand, but let me have a think about it. Let's meet for lunch next Saturday to talk things over.*

And there, effectively, the conversation ended.

Table 1: Income and expenditure for first year

Income:		£
From Dawsons		216,000
From Rowans		144,000
Other sales		54,000
Advisory services		13,500
	Total	427,500

Expenditure:		
Materials		140,000
Salaries		140,000
Other expenditure		45,000
	Total	325,000

Table 2: Projected income and expenditure for second year

Income:		£
From Dawsons		270,000
From Rowans		162,000
Other sales		71,000
Advisory services		63,000
	Total	566,000

Expenditure:		
Materials		158,000
Salaries		184,000
Other expenditure		72,000
	Total	414,000

Learning objectives

Underlying the discussion of the Holmesafe case are two main learning objectives. These are firstly to introduce students to SWOT analysis,[1] and secondly to introduce the issue of business ethics. Students are introduced, at an early stage in the course, to the fact that business decisions are based not only on rational economic analysis but also on intuition, gut-feel and the political realities of a situation.

The SWOT framework is a fairly straightforward one. It may be introduced in a short lecture, after which students are invited to apply it to a case situation. (*Here is a concept, apply it to this situation and come back with some conclusions, i.e. using an input – discovery – reflection sequence of learning modes.*)

However, an alternative approach is to guide students in a case discussion *during which they discover* the SWOT framework through the analysis and discussion of a particular situation. They then recognise the wider, general applicability of the framework (*i.e. discovery – reflection*). If, with some effort, students can discover something for themselves rather than being told about it first then, in my experience, they gain a sense of ownership of that discovery. By investing energy and making a discovery, learning becomes more exciting and development is enhanced.

[1] Strengths, Weaknesses, Opportunities and Threats: a widely used framework for summarising internal and external factors that affect an organisation's strategic situation.

The discussion

A case discussion can be thought of as having three phases:

1   Opening, orientation phase.
2   Middle phase, exploring the main issues in the case.
3   Closing phase, summarising issues, reinforcing key learning points.

We will examine each of these stages in turn in relation to the Holmesafe case.

Opening the discussion

Motivation, as all teachers know, is an essential prerequisite for learning. So the teacher's first task is to capture the learner's interest. We work to create in our students a need to know and a wish to explore and discover. We can create these conditions in a number of ways. We do so initially in our first meetings with students and as a result of the relationships we establish with them.

For effective case sessions we need to use material that students find relevant, interesting and readable.[2] We should also have student motivation in mind in deciding how to open a case discussion.

Our opening comments or questions should aim to get all students personally engaged with the case situation. How might we begin the discussion? Should we make some general introductory comments about the case? Should we start by asking a question? If so should the

---

[2] More than 15,000 cases are accessible through The European Case Clearing House (ECCH). Its on-line search facility helps searchers meet their specific case requirements.

question be directed at one particular student or to all of them? Our decisions on these points will depend in part on how well we know the student group. A challenging opening question to one particular student may be appropriate if we know the group well, but could be seen as overly aggressive by a group we are teaching for the first time.

One way in which the involvement of all students can be achieved from the outset is to pose a question and ask *all* students to jot down a brief response. Several students can then be invited to share their responses with the class. Discussion and debate are usually enhanced when there are differing views about issues within a case. So, if the opening question to the class is one to which opposing, but equally valid, responses are possible, the discussion is likely to be more lively.

A useful question with which to open discussion of the Holmesafe case is:

> How well has Holmesafe performed to date?

All students are asked to score Holmesafe's performance on a scale of 1 to 10. Their scores are then compared and the discussion begins by asking those who gave particularly high or low scores to say something about the criteria they used to arrive at their scores.

Middle phase

This occupies about 40 minutes of the one hour scheduled for discussion of the case. The following summary indicates how the session normally develops.

Discussion is initially focussed on Holmesafe's past *performance* (prompted by the opening question) and present *position*, triggered perhaps by asking:

> How well placed do you think Holmesafe is to face the future?

As these questions are explored opportunities naturally arise to consider what Holmesafe is good at, where it seems to be vulnerable and so on. The answers to these questions form the basis of the SWOT framework that students are building for themselves as the discussion proceeds.

Shaping questions that guide the processes of analysis and discovery is a key skill of the case teacher. The kinds of questions used by case teachers and what they are designed to achieve were discussed in Section 1.4.

The possibility of losing its major customer is a major threat to Holmesafe and fairly obvious to students. Less obvious to some students are the ethical issues implicit in Jackson's phone call to Holmes. The tutor can move the discussion on to this theme by asking a question along the lines of:

> What do you make of Jackson's phone call to Holmes?

There are several possible interpretations, and these should be noted as students offer them. These conflicting views on the phone call, and the range of responses open to Jackson as a result, are central issues in the case and a rich source of potential learning.

The nature of the dilemma faced by Holmes can be probed by asking such questions as:

How big a problem is this?

Is it an operational or policy/strategy matter?

How important is the decision Holmes must make, for the future of the business?

Discussion of what action Holmes should take can be triggered by asking students:

What would you now do if in Holmes's position?

This question can be expanded by asking them to consider immediate, short-term and longer term actions.

Closing the discussion

As the session progresses student comments are noted on the chalkboard (or equivalent) in such a way that they provide a reasonably structured summary of the session. Although we may have a desired board summary in mind from the outset, the summary arrived at by the end of the session should not appear contrived. Students will accept some rephrasing of their observations but highly selective recording and editing of their contributions will be resented and will undermine the session's effectiveness.

For the Holmesafe case the board summary might include some analysis of the financial data from the case, and perhaps diagrams showing bases for strategic decisions and a SWOT summary, similar to those shown below.

Strengths	Weaknesses
Good sales growth	Undue reliance on major customer
Good profit margins	Poor marketing?
Good cash flow	Unaware of competition?
Advisory business developing strongly	Careless of relationship with Jackson
Technical innovation?	
Threats	**Opportunities**
Loss of major customer	Security a growth industry
Competition (superiority of competitor's products?)	Greater use of Holmes's inventive skill?
Relationship with Jackson	Broadening of product range
	Broadening of customer base

Bases for strategic decisions

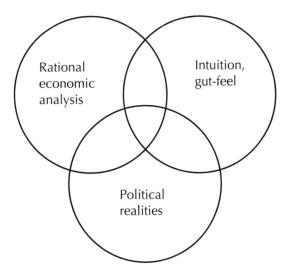

Using case incidents

Although used less widely than the more conventional 'situation case', short case incidents can be a useful teaching vehicle. They can be introduced into a class to illustrate a lecture point, or provide the basis for an exercise. One attraction of the incident is its brevity. It can be issued at any time and read in a few seconds. There may be no need to provide printed copies, since most incidents are short enough to display on an overhead projector or flip-chart. An example incident is shown below.

AN AWKWARD INCIDENT

Mary O'Hara, a training school supervisor, was approached one morning by one of her trainees who was obviously very agitated about something. Pointing to a man leaving the office, the trainee said that she had just seen him searching through the pockets of her coat. The coat was hanging on a rack near the door with several others.

Mary recognised the man leaving the office as the company's maintenance electrician.

She asked the trainee if there was anything missing from her pockets. The trainee said she did not think so.

Mary O'Hara was uncertain what she should now do.

Much of what has already been said about case teaching applies equally to the use of incidents. The following additional comments may be helpful to those who may wish to include case incidents as part of their teaching.

Before considering how this incident might be 'taught' let us stand back for a moment to consider the way in which this incident has been communicated to course members. Is its presentation in written form appropriate? The supervisor in the real incident perceived it only through a few fleeting impressions. A video reconstruction of the incident, played just once, would present course members with a much more realistic 'case' to work on than a written account of it. We will consider alternatives to the written case in part two of this guide.

Returning now to our 'awkward incident', this is used on a problem solving course for first-line supervisors. Before the incident is introduced course members have been preoccupied with more complex problems in which time is available for data collection and analysis, and a structured, planned approach to problem solving seems to pay off. Although the incident appears rather trivial by comparison, the element of urgency within it is of interest. How relevant is a planned approach to problem solving in this situation?

One of the challenges facing the case teacher and case writer is to present a case in such a way that the reader is not impeded by constant reminders that this is just a case. As far as possible we are attempting, with cases, to bring a slice of reality into the classroom. Anything that gets in the way of this obstructs the learning environment we are trying to create. Putting course members into the role of key actors in case situations can help to achieve the 'willing suspension of disbelief' so important to effective case teaching.

So, an obvious question to ask course members is:

What would you do if in this supervisor's shoes?

Typical responses to this question and the kinds of follow-up questions these might provoke are described below and in the next few pages.

1 Go after the man and confront him with the trainee's accusation

In doing this, what precisely would you say to him? Would you tackle him alone or in the company of the trainee? Why (or why not)?

The man might react to the accusation in a number of different ways. For example, he may:

(a) deny the accusation categorically;

(b) admit looking through the coat but explain that he mistook it for his own;

(c) confess and apologise, claiming that it had been an inexplicable lapse on his part.

What would be your response to each of these reactions? Are there any other responses the accused might make? Have you considered the possible attitude of the trainee, and your boss (assuming he learns of the incident) to the way you handle the situation? How might your handling of this issue affect future relationships between you and your trainees, your boss and the accused? Are you likely to be able to resolve this situation yourself, or does it raise wider policy issues?

2 As nothing has been taken, suggest the trainee forgets the incident and remind her not to leave valuables unattended

There are some rogues in most organisations. Reminding subordinates of this fact of life may be all you can reasonably do in this situation, especially as nothing has actually been stolen. You have only one witness who may possibly have misinterpreted the accused's behaviour. What are the risks in taking this view of the situation? Is your subordinate likely to be satisfied with this? Do you have any wider responsibilities in the matter?

Suppose that at some time in the future the accused is found guilty of theft in the organisation and it becomes known that you took no action in the present situation. Could you be criticised for failing to act? Would that criticism be justified?

3 First check with the other people in the office that nothing has been taken from their coats

This response indicates recognition of the importance of information. Obtaining additional information helps to increase understanding of a situation. However, there are several points for discussion arising from this suggestion.

Is this the first thing you would do? Why? What are your priorities? Would you call all your trainees together, or speak to them separately? Why? Would you explain why you are asking them to check their coats, or ask them to do so with no explanation? Are there any risks to the reputation of the accused, if he is subsequently found to be innocent? Once you had asked your trainees to check their belongings what would your next action be, assuming:

(a) nothing is missing?

(b) one trainee tells you his wallet is missing?

4 Seek the advice of my boss before taking further action

Why have you decided on this approach? What assumptions are you making, about the relationship between the supervisor and her boss; about their personalities and management styles? What kind of response would you expect from your boss if you took this approach? What questions do you think your boss would ask about the incident? Have you thought about the answers you would give to these? What assumptions have you made about the supervisor's authority in this situation? What view might the trainee take of your decision to seek advice before acting? What advice do you imagine your boss might give you? What action might he take? Have you considered your attitude towards the advice he might give you or the action he might take?

There are, of course, many other courses of action open to the supervisor in this incident. Whatever action course members propose, get them to think through carefully what outcome their proposals are designed to achieve. Is it intended primarily to safeguard their subordinates' property, punish the guilty, protect the innocent, enhance their own reputation in the eyes of the boss or subordinates? Are their proposals fair to all concerned? What do they mean by fair? Are there any possible consequences of their proposals that are undesirable?

If any course members have witnessed a theft, been accused themselves of theft, or have had their own property stolen, it is likely to have influenced their response to this case incident. Get them to reflect on this. To what extent can we consciously use past experiences as a learning opportunity?

Postscript

The approach adopted above has been to get course members to explain why they would act in the ways they propose, upon what data, opinions, attitudes, and values their proposals are based. Within what constraints have their proposals been formulated? What outcome do they desire, expect, from their proposed action? Have they thought through the proposals to try to identify undesirable outcomes?

Through such discussion it is hoped that course members will develop a deeper understanding of incidents of the kind described, increase their awareness of the basis upon which they themselves act, and become more effective supervisors as a result.

Role playing

Some case studies and case incidents lend themselves well to role playing. Acting out the case study can significantly heighten the understanding, not only of the 'actors', but also of the observers.

If video recording facilities are available the opportunity can be taken of reviewing the role play. Self-analysis by participants of their performance can provide potent learning. What behaviours, on their part, did they consider to be effective, and which were ineffective? How, if at all, would they modify their behaviour if playing the role again? What were their feelings as they acted out the role? Are they able to draw parallels with situations they have faced at work? The observers too can also comment on the role play. What did they observe about the actions and feelings of the participants? With a video replay they can also check out the accuracy of their initial observations.

Short case incidents can provide the basis for productive role play. In the incident shown below, 'Death in the Family', one senses that the supervisor wanted to be supportive but felt unable to do so openly. Here is an opportunity, through role play, to try to overcome inhibitions often felt in expressing feelings and sharing emotions openly.

DEATH IN THE FAMILY

Alan Grimes, a supervisor, had a woman clerk who was much older than himself. He heard on the grapevine that there had been a death in her family. She did not tell him, and he was grateful because he was not sure about how to handle such situations. But he did notice she was more anxious and making more errors. So he discreetly increased his monitoring of her work.

Another incident case, 'The Interview Panel', provides an opportunity for a supervisor to argue her case for being included on an interview panel.

THE INTERVIEW PANEL

Sonia Perry, an accounts office manager, was responsible for several sections, including wages. When this section's supervisor retired Sonia asked her boss if she could be included on the interview panel when it met to appoint a replacement. He refused her request, saying he didn't think she had sufficient experience. Sonia felt this had diminished her authority and when the new supervisor was appointed Sonia left her to run the wages section very much as she wished.

In preparing to role play this incident the student (and his or her course colleagues) could be invited to consider what arguments might persuade the boss of the merits of the request. What would make this a good idea *from the boss's point of view*? The role player should also be encouraged to think through *all* the reasons why he or she *wants* to be included on the panel.

For very few incidents of the kind shown above is it possible to be prescriptive, to say how the supervisor or manager *ought* to have handled the situation. Management is not like that. Some approaches are better than others in certain circumstances, but there are very few *right* approaches in any absolute sense.

Nevertheless, discussion of critical incidents taken from the supervisor's working life, under the guidance of an experienced tutor, has proved effective in heightening understanding, improving skills and developing the supervisor's judgement in the day-to-day performance of his or her job.

Preparing students to learn through cases

Student expectations

Preparing students to learn through case studies seldom gets the attention it should. Course members need to know what the case study approach is designed to achieve and why it is considered the appropriate learning method in a particular course or subject area.

Unless the expectations of course members and their attitudes to different learning methods are properly considered, many learning objectives will remain unfulfilled.

Common complaints about the Case Method

Cases have no unique answer

Information is ambiguous and contradictory

The issue is not stated (*the task may be to identify the issues*)

Information is redundant or irrelevant

The instructor does not solve the case

Case teaching is inefficient

Note taking is difficult

The instructor is non-directive in discussions (*He or she may wish to develop self-reliance*)

If students are to be taught using the case method it seems reasonable that the merits of the method should be explained to them. Indeed, I have found it advantageous with all classes I meet to say something about the teaching–learning partnership and discuss the expectations and obligations of all those involved.

As part of this discussion we examine the nature of learning and draw on the Lancaster model of learning to do so (described earlier in this guide) .

I discuss with students the adverse reactions sometimes expressed by newcomers to case learning, and suggest some 'Dos and Don'ts' for case discussions.

'Dos and Don'ts' for case discussion

Dos	Don'ts
Prepare for class	Make sudden topic changes
Push your ideas	Repeat yourself
Listen to others	Repeat what others say
Keep an open mind	Use unfair hindsight
Relate outside experiences	
Relate past cases in course	
Be provocative	
Bring in outside research	
Summarise	
Recognise flow of discussion	
Be constructive	
Be brief	
Evaluate your own participation	

I point to the fact that 'knowledge is not behaviour'; that managers need to develop both diagnostic and action skills. Through analysing, discussing and drawing conclusions about case situations, and making recommendations on those situations that take account of potential implementation problems, students will be doing much to support the development of both sets of skills.

A discussion with students along the lines indicated above can be supplemented with a note outlining the main features of the case method. Two examples of such notes are included in the appendices to this guide.

Developing your case teaching skills

Leading a case discussion for the first time can be a daunting experience. This is especially so if your preferred teaching style to date has been for predictable, quite tightly structured sessions in which you maintain fairly close control of agenda and process throughout.

Teaching with cases involves rather more risk. The content of the session will be less certain and control must be shared with students. As case teachers we must be prepared to release control into the class during the discussion. However, we must be ready and able to take back control, when appropriate, so that the educational objectives for the session can be achieved.

Sharing control of a session with a class is something that requires practice. Sometimes students will pick up an issue that you think is of only marginal relevance and pursue this with great enthusiasm. It can be difficult in such circumstances to regain control of the discussion. This is where a degree of panic can set in! If you try to wrest back control too obviously it can be counterproductive and resented by the students. They will be reluctant to pursue the core issues that you believe are more important. It is usually better to allow the discussion to go where students want to take it, at least for a while. Try to decide what it is that has captured student interest in this issue. As the discussion continues look for opportunities to frame a question that is clearly rooted in the present area of interest, but provides a credible, yet not too obvious, route back to the core issues on which you want students to focus.

A range of questions is available to discussion leaders that are helpful in shaping and guiding case sessions in the direction necessary to meet learning objectives (see Section 1.4). The degree to which the case teacher should impose direction upon the discussion is open to debate. My own view is that teaching is rather akin to taking people on a journey. We have a route and destination in mind, but along that route there will be opportunities for local exploration and discovery by individuals and groups. Eventually, however, we have to get them back on the bus, or we won't be home in time for tea!

If you are a newcomer to case teaching it might not be a good idea to 'dive in at the deep end' straight away. Spend a little time first in the 'shallow end' to gain confidence. Start your case teaching in a small way. Use a short case or incident within your normal teaching session to illustrate or supplement the main lesson. Tell students why you think this will be a useful part of the session. Ask students for feedback after the class. As confidence grows more detailed cases can be introduced and more control can be relinquished to class members.

Take care in selecting the cases you use. Will they capture the interest of your students? Are the issues you wish to cover in your course key issues in the case? Choose cases that have accompanying teaching notes if you can. But do your own detailed analysis of the case before looking at the analysis in the teaching note. Is the case too difficult for your students, or too easy?

The difficulty faced by students in tackling cases is due to three main factors. These are: (i) the analytical task facing the student, (ii) the concepts or techniques being addressed and (iii) the presentation of the case material in terms of its volume and clarity. In the diagram below these factors are shown on a three-dimensional grid (Erskine *et al.*, 1981). Examples of increasing difficulty under each of these three headings are also shown below.

Case difficulty

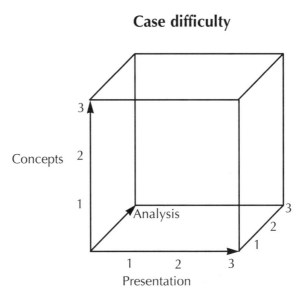

Analysis

1   This is what the manager did. What do you think of it? Does the decision match the problem? Why/why not?

2   This is the decision facing the manager. What would you do if you were in his or her shoes and why?

3   Here is some information about some
    individuals in an organisation. Do you think
    they have problems, need to make some
    decisions, or set some policies? If so, which,
    why, how and when?

Concepts

1   Almost all students will grasp it with a
    minimum of additional explanation, e.g.
    chain of command, ratio analysis, 'push or
    pull' promotion.

2   Needs further explanation through class
    discussion or lecturette. May involve a
    combination of simple concepts, e.g.
    return on investment, economic order
    quantity, authority versus responsibility.

3   Needs extensive clarification via lecture or
    other means. Possible that some students,
    even then, will not fully understand. Could
    be a combination of several concepts, e.g.
    cost of capital, pricing, motivation.

Presentation

1   Amount of material required for analysis
    relatively small. Minimum amount of
    extraneous material. Relatively short case.

2   Some extraneous information is given. Case
    length average.

3   Considerable extraneous information. Long
    case or a tough case because of missing
    information.

Much can be learned about the core skills of case teaching by observing experienced case teachers in action. If you have colleagues in this category ask them if they will let you sit in on some of their sessions. Invite them into your own case classes, and seek their feedback on the session.

If there are no experienced case teachers in your institution, a useful substitute might be a video of experienced case teachers in action with their classes. ECCH has produced such videos in the past and will be able to advise on what is currently available in this area.

The observation and discussion of other case teachers' work can be immensely valuable, but the skills of case teaching can only be developed through practise (i.e. learning by discovery through action and feedback). Sometimes, however, feedback is limited to what we are able to pick up ourselves. Additional constructive feedback from others may not be readily available in your organisation. Fortunately, however, support is available for newcomers to case teaching from outside sources.

ECCH organises case teaching workshops on a regular basis. Many of these provide opportunities for new case teachers to lead practice sessions in which their workshop colleagues act as 'students'. Constructive feedback on these sessions is provided by tutors and workshop members. ECCH workshops thus provide a non-threatening risk-free environment in which to practise case teaching and on which to receive helpful advice.

U sing case studies in examinations

Cases are used in teaching to provide *opportunities for learning*. In examinations they are used for a rather different purpose; here they provide opportunities for students to *demonstrate their learning*.

A case study typically contains a wide range of issues. Its use as a vehicle for ongoing assessment or final examination must therefore be planned with care.

The essential first stage in this process is to be very clear about what it is that we wish to assess. What knowledge, skills, or attitudes do we want the student to demonstrate?

The questions below identify a number of issues that need to be thought through in order to clarify assessment objectives, and to decide on the most appropriate method of assessment. If a case study examination seems the most appropriate then these questions will also help us to select a suitable case.

Assessment objectives

Do we want descriptions, explanations, predictions?

Do we want students to demonstrate:

Awareness of / acquaintance with X?

Knowledge of X? To what depth and breadth?

Ability to identify and bring together relevant data?

Ability to analyse that data?

Competence in the use of specific methods or techniques of analysis?

Perception, ability to draw inferences?

Judgemental skills in the face of inadequate data?

Creativity in formulating recommendations for action?

Recognition of the problems that might arise in implementing the recommendation?

Presentation and communication skills?

Traditionally, assignments or examinations are in written form, but it might be worth considering whether this is the appropriate mode. How, other than in writing, might students demonstrate their development?

The amount of guidance students need concerning case examinations and assignments will depend to some extent on the stage they have reached in their course and their maturity. Case examination questions must be worded with precision; there is normally no opportunity for clarification in an examination as there would be during a case discussion.

The wording of questions may be varied to suit different student groups as shown below.

Wording examination questions

(a) Evaluate the proposed strategy of X.

Here the student must know of and select a suitable framework or approach and demonstrate ability to use it.

(b) Using the J and S Strategy Evaluation framework, evaluate the proposed strategy of X.

Here the student is directed to a specific framework and must demonstrate ability to use it.

(c) Using the J and S Strategy Evaluation framework, evaluate the proposed strategy of X under the headings of suitability, feasibility and acceptability.

Here the student is directed to a specific framework and given headings to remind him or her of its features, and must demonstrate ability to use it.

Part Two

WRITING
Case studies

Case development

We have seen, in Part One, what jobs we want cases to do in the classroom. Now we turn to the task of writing cases to do these jobs.

The case development process is broadly as shown below, and we shall explore each of these stages in turn.

Case development

1   Data collection

   Need-specific versus 'trawling'

2   Data restructuring

   Deciding the structure, writing and editing the case

3   Case enhancement

   (a)   *Supplementary material – printed word, audio, video*

   (b)   *Teaching note*

Case data comes from a variety of sources, and for convenience these may be categorised as follows:

1   Field researched – based on interviews and observations in a host organisation;

2   Desk researched – based on company reports, newspaper or magazine articles, TV programmes;

3   Armchair cases – based on the writer's own experience.

The classic case is written as a result of field research. However many successful teaching cases are based entirely on desk research, and cases written on the basis of the writer's own personal experiences can sometimes be effective.

Field research

Field research is undertaken when the case writer or researcher wishes to record what is actually happening within an organisation, and the views of those involved about the organisation's present and past situation. If cases are to bring a slice of reality into the classroom and reflect current issues as seen by those taking part in them, rather than the views of external commentators, then field research is the means to this.

Data is gathered by observing the organisation's activities and talking to its staff. The case writer may have been attracted to the organisation as a result of developments within the organisation or problems it faces, and about which he or she has become aware. This initial awareness may suggest to the case writer that the organisation faces issues that could usefully be included and discussed within teaching programmes.

Before embarking on field research it is important to be clear about what you want to do, and how to do it. If you are a newcomer to case research you may find it helpful to work through the questionnaire on case research preparation in Appendix 1.

Establishing a relationship with a subject organisation

Once a potential host has been identified, gaining the cooperation of the organisation becomes the case writer's key task. This needs to be handled with care. Why should an organisation open its doors to a researcher, spend time discussing its operations, problems, or whatever it is that the researcher wants to enquire about? Fundamentally there is a selling job that needs to be done to persuade a subject organisation that their cooperation is worth while.

Sometimes the initial trigger for a case comes from a news item. If this comes from a press release and involves developments a company wishes to publicise, this can be a useful basis on which to make an initial contact. You can express interest in the company's development and request more information. Mention the importance of students being made aware of the latest developments, or best practice, of the kind revealed in the news item. Try to obtain an interview with someone at the organisation in order to supplement the news item.

The process of initiating a fruitful relationship with a host organisation is a challenging one. At the centre of this is the need to make things as easy as possible for the host. Managers need to know about the demands you are likely to make upon them and be reassured on questions of confidentiality and the content of the case. Case writers should always give a categoric undertaking that no information they obtain from the host organisation will be revealed to others, and that the case produced will not be released until the host organisation has given its written approval.

Approval to undertake field research should always be sought at senior level in the host organisation. Many case writers have found their work wasted when approval obtained at middle manager level is later rescinded at senior level.

If an interview is granted do your homework before-hand. Don't waste your contact's time by asking questions about matters that are readily available in published sources. Prepare an action plan before you go. The first meeting may be with someone who is not in a position to approve your request for research access. If so, one of your tasks will be to gain access to and/or approval at more senior level. A short written document setting out what you want to do and why, and the educational value you attach to the company's contribution, may be helpful to your contact if he or she is persuaded to take your request higher.

Gathering data in the host organisation

If you are granted access for research inside the organisa-tion use your time to gather data that is not available else-where. Keep your demands on the time of respondents to a minimum. Your respondents need to know something about you and the purpose of your research. They need to trust you and be reassured on matters of confidentiality. If they tell you something in confidence then this must be preserved. Don't start with difficult questions. Try to relax the respondent. Don't talk down to respondents and don't use academic jargon. Don't talk too much. Let respon-dents do the talking.

Although you may have certain aims in mind for the interview, and your opening questions will be designed with these in mind, don't force respondents to follow your predetermined agenda. Invaluable insights are often obtained by letting respondents talk about things of their choosing. Listening skills are important. Give respondents time to gather their thoughts or to pluck up courage to confide in you. Wait for their responses. Don't rush in with a supplementary question to fill a silence.

Although the case writer may be seeking material to meet a specific teaching need, once access is gained to an organisation, avenues of interest can become apparent that were totally unexpected at the outset. In this way one may discover rich and unexpected material for the current case or reveal opportunities for further cases that explore quite different issues. This is akin to trawling or prospecting – not quite knowing what may be discovered. So, in summary, case data may be obtained both through need-specific research and may also reveal itself through serendipity.

Taking notes

Taking notes during an interview presents certain problems. It should not be obtrusive. The purposeful noting of private conversations can be a little intimidating. A small tape recorder can overcome the problem, but again can be seen as intrusive. Once initial contact and trust have been established, however, a respondent may be quite willing to allow the use of a recorder.

An alternative is to take a colleague with you so that one person can ask questions while the other takes notes. However, this is costly in researcher time and can be intimidating if a single respondent faces two interviewers.

Write up the notes as soon after the interview as possible, while it is still fresh in the mind. You may also wish to make a note of non-verbal aspects of the interview that throw light on relevant aspects.

Problem areas

Most organisations like to recount their successes and are pleased for these to be reported in a case. However, organisational failures can often provide more useful learning than success stories. But these can be difficult to research because host organisations are reluctant to reveal their shortcomings. They will be least likely to do so at the time of a crisis. However, if a successful recovery is made, they may be quite willing to talk, after the event, about how they turned things around. You may want the focus of your case to be upon these past problems. However, this could make the case rather dated by the time it is written up and released for class use. You will have to consider whether this will have any adverse effect on the case in terms of its relevance or acceptability to students. We will discuss how dates and times can be incorporated into a case in Section 2.5.

Confidential, sensitive or embarrassing information presents problems for the host organisation and the case writer. One way around this is to disguise the case in some way so that its identity is not known to the reader. This is sometimes done to secure the release of a valuable teaching case that the subject company is otherwise unwilling to release. However, if the organisation is distinctive in some way, in terms of its products, services or market position, then disguise can be difficult. If a case is regarded as so good that disguise is justified, care should be taken that the disguise used does not distort the case to the point where its value as a learning vehicle is undermined. More will be said later about the formal aspects of case release, i.e. obtaining permission from the subject organisation for its publication.

Variations on a theme

Although the field research we are discussing here focuses on the task of researching and writing a conventional situation or decision case, field research may be involved in the preparation of other types of case.

For example, the small incidents used as examples in this guide are taken from a field research project into the training needs of office supervisors. This gathered 180 critical incidents reported by supervisors as indicative of the day-to-day problems they faced.

More ambitious case research projects may involve, for example, the preparation of a series of related cases on a number of companies competing in the same industry sector, together with an explanatory note on the sector. In such circumstances the issue of trust between host organisations and case researchers becomes even more important.

Briefing research assistants

If you are fortunate enough to have some help with the data collection process it is important to brief the research assistant adequately. If researchers are inexperienced they need to be made aware of the importance of sensitivity, confidentiality and the related issues outlined above. It is likely that they will be introduced to the host organisation by the leader of the research project, and will observe how the leader, as role model, establishes rapport within the host organisation.

A written brief for a research assistant is worth while even for small, relatively informal projects. An example is shown in Appendix 2.

Desk-based and armchair cases

Although cases based on desk research are regarded by some academics as inferior to field researched cases, desk research can often provide sufficient data from which to write an effective teaching case. It can also be very cost effective compared with field research.

Although we are differentiating here between field and desk researched cases, most field researched cases also incorporate some desk research. In reality there is a continuum running from totally field researched to totally desk researched cases.

Desk-based cases

Desk researched cases are frequently based on newspaper and journal reports. Usually several different reports are obtained of the same events to provide the case writer with a number of different perspectives.

Particularly rich sources of case data are the Offer for Sale documents of companies being floated on the stock market. These usually contain detailed accounts of the origins and development of the company, information on its directors, its recent performance and an outline of its future strategy. In addition, when a company 'goes public' there will be further information in the business press. This may include business commentators' views on the firm's prospects and personnel. Taken together, this data may provide all the raw material needed for a case. Even so, once the case is written up, the subject organisation may be willing to comment upon it. If so, this can lead to additional insights being incorporated into the case. Thereby it acquires some elements of a field researched case at minimum inconvenience to both the case writer and organisation concerned. Additional information of this kind can often be obtained when permission is sought for case release (see later).

The reader may wonder, at this point, why the material collected through desk research should not be given to students as it stands. Why work it up into a conventional case study? Sometimes collected news items and journal articles are issued to students in their original format, and to good effect. More often, though, the case writer wants to be selective in what is included in the case for good educational reasons. For example, we may want to filter out the opinions of journalists in order that students can reach their own conclusions on case issues. We shall have more to say on this point when we discuss data selection and case structure in Section 2.5.

Armchair cases

These are so called because they involve no field or desk research on the part of the writer, but can be composed entirely from the comfort of an armchair. They are based upon the writer's own past experiences. Lessons learned by the writer in the course of a business or academic career may seem to offer an appropriate basis for teaching cases. Sometimes they do, and armchair cases can be effective. However, they are generally regarded as inferior to field or desk researched cases, principally for two reasons.

As they are based on the *past* experiences of the writer, they are inevitably dated. Consequently they do not reflect issues *currently* faced by organisations, which it can be argued is an important ingredient of a good teaching case. It is also difficult to ensure internal consistency within an armchair case, unless it is quite short. A further shortcoming is that the case is likely to be written up on the basis of one person's perception of a situation or events, i.e. that of the case writer. Despite these shortcomings, for a case incident, or very short case study, armchair reflections can sometimes be the source of useful teaching material.

Writing the case draft

To a large extent the case writer's task is one of data selection and restructuring. The restructuring involves the telling of a story within which there are discoveries to be made and things to be learned. In some ways a case study is like a detective story. Things happen and it is not always clear why or how they happened. There are clues to be gathered and juggled with, pieces of a jigsaw to be identified and put into place. Slowly, as evidence is collected and considered, the situation becomes clearer. It becomes possible to see the broad picture and the critical points within it, and reflect on what might have been.

Case writing also has parallels with investigative journalism. What tensions exist behind a company's carefully cultivated public image? What might we usefully learn from events as varied as the Cuban missile crisis, Watergate and the collapse of Robert Maxwell's empire?

Although case writing includes elements of both these genre, it can be regarded as a literary form in its own right.

Making a start

This can be the most difficult stage in writing a case. If we worry too much at the outset about the finer aspects of style and structure we may find it very hard to write anything. For many case writers the first draft is very rough, and little more than a 'data dump'. But just getting the raw material down can get things moving, and provide something to rework, structure and then fine tune. In broad terms a case can be thought of as having three main sections, as shown below.

Case draft

Opening: Create interest, provide orientation

Middle: Bring out key issues

Closure: Summarise key issues, need for solution
            to problems, constraints on solutions

It can be helpful to start by drafting an outline, perhaps using the three headings above. Your word processor may provide an outlining facility to facilitate this approach. Some writers use a simple network diagram to keep time scales and the linkages between different case issues clear in their minds. Once a case outline or network diagram has been prepared work can start on fleshing out each section. Often the opening and closing sections, which require special consideration, are left until last, and the early work concentrates on developing the main issues in the middle section of the case.

To illustrate the process we will trace the development of a short case study through its various stages.

Case drafting example

Midborough Technical College

The case describes a fairly mundane administrative problem in a further education college. This is not riveting stuff but can nevertheless be used to illustrate some basic points of case drafting. The outline prepared for the case is shown below.

Outline for Midborough Technical College

Synopsis

A senior lecturer in a local technical college is faced with the problem of arranging substitute lecturers when staff are off sick

Opening

Create interest by indicating the need for action

Middle section – main case issues

Case actor(s) and their roles

Case context: Something about the organisation in which the case takes place

More specific information relating to the main case issues: (a) time constraints, (b) difficulties in locating staff, (c) organisational climate

Close

Actor's aims and values

Reminder of the problem he faces

The case developed from this outline is shown below. Read the case through and spend a few minutes thinking about what job each paragraph is doing. What part does each paragraph play in the case as a whole? Does each paragraph make a worthwhile contribution to the case? Consider, too, the target audience for the case. To whom might the case be of interest?

MIDBOROUGH TECHNICAL COLLEGE

It was a little after 9a.m. and Alan Knight, a senior lecturer in the Engineering Department of Midborough Technical College, put down the phone and turned to consult the staff timetables above his desk. Julie Monro's husband had just telephoned to say that his wife would be unable to take her scheduled class at 10.00a.m. that morning as she was sick and was likely to be away from college for three or four days.

Alan Knight was responsible to his Head of Department for all matters concerning class and staff timetables and during the winter months he had frequently to deal with the problem of finding replacements for staff who were sick.

The Engineering Department, the largest of the college's seven teaching departments, provided a variety of craft and technician courses on a part-time day and evening basis. The teaching staff of the department, some 35 strong, tended to specialise in one of three broad subject areas: Engineering Drawing, Engineering Science and Mathematics or Workshop Practice. Staff were expected to attend the college for ten sessions each week, a session being a morning, afternoon or evening. During this time they taught for 18 to 23 hours, depending on their lectureship grade. When not in class, staff were engaged on lesson preparation, marking and administrative duties of various kinds.

The college telephonist came on duty just before 9.00a.m., at which time most day classes began. Alan Knight was not on the telephone at home and consequently he sometimes had to find a substitute for a sick colleague at very short notice.

A look through staff timetables would locate one or more lecturers likely to be available at the time required and having selected someone whose subject area was appropriate, Knight would attempt to contact him or her on the internal telephone. However, since preparation and administrative duties were performed at various locations throughout the widely dispersed college, locating the required lecturer was not always easy. Those lecturers who did their preparation in staff rooms were clearly most accessible, and more likely to be asked to deputise for absent colleagues at short notice, even in a subject area that they did not normally teach.

In less urgent cases, substitutes for sick lecturers were arranged by means of a memo. This would be left in the substitute's pigeon-hole located in the staff common room. On occasions, however, these notes would remain uncollected, the lecturers concerned claiming that they had not visited the common room during the period concerned.

For some time Alan Knight had been considering how he could improve this situation. He wanted to ensure a fair distribution of any additional workload and at the same time reduce the frustration he often experienced in dealing with this problem.

The following diagram shows the structure of the Midborough Technical College case study. The figure also poses some specific questions about the structure and wording of the case. Spend a few minutes comparing the points made in the figure with any views you formed when you read the case for the first time.

MIDBOROUGH TECHNICAL COLLEGE

How relevant?

1 Establishes a situation in which action is required.

It was a little after 9a.m. and Alan Knight, a senior lecturer in the Engineering Department of Midborough Technical College, put down the phone and turned to consult the staff timetables above his desk. Julie Monro's husband had just telephoned to say that his wife would be unable to take her scheduled class at 10.00a.m. that morning as she was sick and was likely to be away from college for three or four days.

2 Establishes Knight's role in the situation.

Alan Knight was responsible to his Head of Department for all matters concerning class and staff timetables and during the winter months he had frequently to deal with the problem of finding replacements for staff who were sick.

How often? Do we need to know his other duties and responsibilities?

3 Establishes the context. But what is relevant? Does this information aid an understanding of the case situation?

The Engineering Department, the largest of the college's seven teaching departments, provided a variety of craft and technician courses on a part-time day and evening basis. The teaching staff of the department, some 35 strong, tended to specialise in one of three broad subject areas: Engineering Drawing, Engineering Science and Mathematics or Workshop Practice. Staff were expected to attend the college for ten sessions each week, a session being a morning, afternoon or evening. During this time they taught for 18 to 23 hours, depending on their lectureship grade. When not in class, staff were engaged on lesson preparation, marking and administrative duties of various kinds.

4 Urgency due to lack of phone. Is the solution too obvious?

The college telephonist came on duty just before 9.00a.m., at which time most day classes began. Alan Knight was not on the telephone at home and consequently he sometimes had to find a substitute for a sick colleague at very short notice.

5 Describes normal procedures and indicates/ hints at the limitation of these.

A look through staff timetables would locate one or more lecturers likely to be available at the time required and having selected someone whose subject area was appropriate, Knight would attempt to contact him or her on the internal telephone. However, since preparation and administrative duties were performed at various locations throughout the widely dispersed college, locating the required lecturer was not always easy. Those lecturers who did their preparation in staff rooms were clearly most accessible, and more likely to be asked to deputise for absent colleagues at short notice, even in a subject area that they did not normally teach.

Consider the effect of eliminating the above paragraph on understanding the situation.

6 A key paragraph. Indicates the organisational climate?

In less urgent cases, substitutes for sick lecturers were arranged by means of a memo. This would be left in the substitute's pigeon-hole located in the staff common room. On occasions, however, these notes would remain uncollected, the lecturers concerned claiming that they had not visited the common room during the period concerned.

Choice of word? Consider the effect of using 'stating', 'protesting', as alternatives.

7 Establishes Knight's aims and values.

For some time Alan Knight had been considering how he could improve this situation. He wanted to ensure a fair distribution of any additional workload and at the same time reduce the frustration he often experienced in dealing with this problem.

Other sequencing of paragraphs might be used. What would be the effect?

Now that you have read the case and the comments made on its content and structure, how do you think it might be improved? Spend a few minutes thinking about this and jot down a few suggestions. You may also find it useful, before continuing with the next section, to work through Exercise 1 at the end of this guide.

Case structure

How do we construct a case, linking the various issues within it, so that it is interesting to the reader, readable, coherent and also achieves our intended teaching and learning objectives? There are innumerable guides for writers, but very few specifically for writers of cases.

So what form of writing is closest to case writing? Cases are not journal articles, technical papers or reports although they may contain elements of all of these. Perhaps the detective story is the closest parallel. But the case is a distinct literary form and presents particular challenges to its writer.

A framework for structuring cases that has proved helpful to many case writers is that proposed by Harvard's Malcolm P. McNair (1972). He regarded a case as incorporating the four structures summarised below.

> **Case structure**
>
> *Narrative structure*
>
> The flow of events in an unfolding story
>
> *Plot structure*
>
> The element of drama – the clash of people and ideas
>
> *Time structure*
>
> The clear time sequence of events
>
> *Expository structure*
>
> The disclosure, unearthing, communication of information

Let us consider each of these elements in a little more detail.

Narrative

> *An account, often chronological, of a sequence of events, a story.*

The first task in writing a case is to tell a story, to present an interesting and readable account, to describe events and circumstances, both past and present, concerning the subject organisation. The case should be written so that the narrative flows easily, so that the reader is soon immersed in the unfolding story.

We should try to encourage in the reader a 'willing suspension of disbelief'. We need to avoid elements within the case that obstruct the unfolding story. We want the reader to forget that this is just another case study.

Plot

A story line, a plan, a scheme, intrigue.

The plot structure is perhaps the aspect of a case that most closely parallels the detective story. A case needs an element of drama to capture the reader's interest. It must have one or more issues within it that engage the reader's attention.

There is usually a central theme or issue within a case – the main story line or plot – together with a number of subplots that have some kind of impact or influence on one another and on the major issue(s) in the case. These may concern the different motivations and actions of the various 'actors' in a situation and their impact on or contribution to the course of events.

Telling stories

Stories matter. They are where we lose ourselves in order to risk other possibilities, where we can escape and play, or confront and confess.

We do not listen to stories; we join in.

And in accompanying the players of that story we meet many sides of ourselves that we can take back to our lives when the playing is over.

But good stories need to be told well if they are to envelop us. Flair, humour, truth and insight are all tools that must be well honed.

Source: Clark (1996).

Time structure

Chronology, historical sequence.

It is often necessary to know when things happened in a case, so it is important that the time sequence of events is clear. If the case events are narrated in straightforward chronological order there may be no problem about this. But if there are several subplots about events that occurred over parallel periods, confusion may arise.

A 'flashback' technique is sometimes used in cases to add drama or interest to a case. For example, a current problem may be highlighted at the beginning of the case and the flashback approach used to describe the chain of events that led up to this. If this is done it is especially important to check through the time structure of the case during final editing to ensure that dates and times are clear.

It is best to avoid the present tense in case writing (unless this is within reported speech). Even if a case is used with students very soon after it is written the events it describes will have happened in the past. Many cases are used for several years after the date of the events they describe. So the use of words such as 'now', 'this year', 'currently', 'recently' is usually inappropriate. Instead it is better to refer to actual dates. For example, use *'The company launched XYZ product in April 1996'*, rather than *'The company launched XYZ product six months ago'*.

The use of the past tense can sound odd if a case describes an organisation still operating at the time of the case discussion. For example, if students read *'ABC company was based in Dublin and manufactured a range of health food products'*, and know that the firm is still in business, the past tense may seem a little strange. The problem can be minimised by rewording the sentence slightly. For example, '*ABC company, based in Dublin, manufactured a range of health food products*', or '*Its Dublin location gave health food manufacturer ABC company easy access to its main markets*'. Although the past tense is still used in these alternatives it is less obvious than in the original sentence.

Exposition

Discovery, breakthrough, revelation, unearthing.

This is perhaps the most important and challenging aspect of the case writer's task. In Part One we discussed the process of learning through discovery. If as a result of purposeful exploration we make a discovery, then we tend to have a sense of ownership of that discovery or learning. As case writers we need to provide opportunities for students to learn through discovery. So we have to build an expository structure that makes this possible.

This can be likened to opening the curtains on a situation by a predetermined amount. In writing a teaching case we have to throw sufficient light on the situation for the discovery to be possible, but not pull open the curtains too far. If we make the things we want students to find so obvious that no exploration is necessary, then the opportunity for discovery will be lost. In a nutshell, we have to decide what to make explicit and what to place more subtly within the case so that students need to dig a little before it is unearthed. This is a little like the placing of clues in a detective story.

The following illustration examines the Holmesafe Ltd case, discussed in Part One, in terms of the McNair framework. In this short case the narrative, plot and time structures are all quite straightforward. It is the expository structure that newcomers to case writing find most challenging, so it may be helpful to read the underlying rationale for the expository structure in the Holmesafe case.

HOLMESAFE LTD

Narrative structure

1 Origins of business.

Three years ago George Holmes, an engineer, hit upon an idea for a novel security device and produced a successful prototype in his workshop. He made some enquiries through friends to try to find a buyer and was introduced to Frank Jackson, a buyer for the wholesale company of Dawsons Ltd.

2 Key 'actors' introduced.

Jackson offered to discuss the marketing of the product with his immediate superior, Harry Thomas, who was the chief buyer with Dawsons. A meeting was arranged between the three men at which Holmes had a chance to form an opinion of the characters of Jackson and Thomas. He judged that Thomas was a somewhat distant man of high integrity who was prepared to leave action to his more vigorous subordinate Jackson, whose influence with Thomas appeared to be considerable. On the other hand, Holmes felt that Jackson was warm, unscrupulous where the interests of his company, and possibly himself, were concerned, and very active in furthering a cause in which he was interested.

3 Early success and growth.

A trial batch of the devices was made for Dawsons and these were easily sold. Further quantities were made and sold in the same way and by the end of the first three months it became clear that the demand for the product was going to increase. There was also an increase in demand for an advisory service on the installation of the new device and more generally on the problems of electronic security. With the demand on his time increasing, Holmes recruited first one friend, and then two more and between them they were able to manage the business on a part-time basis for the first year. Holmes spent some time cultivating Jackson, and generally being as friendly and affable as circumstances permitted. In turn, Jackson assisted Holmes by pushing sales of the new product and, just as important, ensured that Dawsons paid all bills promptly.

4 Company formation and its relationship with Jackson.

The first year's 'trading' produced good results and the four friends celebrated with a theatre and supper party to which Jackson and his wife were invited, and they made a present of a case of whisky to Jackson. Sales continued to increase and the four decided to form a company, Holmesafe Ltd, with themselves as directors. They asked Jackson to become the fifth director. When he mentioned this to Thomas the latter pointed out that as Jackson would be purchasing goods for Dawsons from Holmesafe this would involve a conflict of interests for him. Jackson recognised the force of this argument and with expressions of regret he turned down the invitation to become a director of Holmesafe.

5 Further growth. Attention drawn to Year 1 results and Year 2 projections.

During their first year of operation as a limited company it became clear that the market had been underestimated. Dawsons' demands were greater than anticipated and a large retail chain also took a substantial volume of goods. Sales to smaller companies also became appreciable and fees from the advisory service also increased. The company could no longer manage on a part-time basis and an old school friend of Holmes became the company's first full-time employee. Half-way through the year a contract was signed with a large national building contractor for Holmesafe to provide an advisory service on home security. Later in the year the company moved into new rented premises and took on a full-time secretary. Income and expenditure for Holmesafe's first year of operations are shown in Table 1.

Table 2 shows the company's projected income and expenditure for the second year of operation.

About mid-way through the second year Holmes received a phone call from Jackson which, after the usual greetings, proceeded as follows:

6 Telephone conversation between Holmes and Jackson.

Jackson: *I thought I'd better let you know that I'm coming under increasing pressure to buy security devices from Browns. They are very similar in performance to yours. Browns have improved their manufacturing methods and are now extremely competitive and very reliable.*

Holmes: *But surely our reputation is worth a great deal. You have put a lot of effort into this yourself and it would be a pity if it were all wasted.*

Jackson: *Sure, and I'll obviously do what I can. But I thought I should let you know how the land lies. Incidentally, there is a bit of personal advice I'd like from you. You remember I used to play in a band a few evenings a week? Well, for personal reasons I have had to give that up and it has left me a bit short of cash. So I'm looking for an evening job that will bring me in a few pounds a week. Got any ideas?*

Holmes: *I don't know of anything offhand, but let me have a think about it. Let's meet for lunch next Saturday to talk things over.*

And there, effectively, the conversation ended.

7 Year 1 Income and expenditure (actual).

Table 1: Income and expenditure for first year

Income:	£
From Dawsons	216,000
From Rowans	144,000
Other sales	54,000
Advisory services	13,500
Total	427,500
Expenditure:	
Materials	140,000
Salaries	140,000
Other expenditure	45,000
Total	325,000

Table 2: Projected income and expenditure for second year	
Income:	£
From Dawsons	270,000
From Rowans	162,000
Other sales	71,000
Advisory services	63,000
Total	566,000
Expenditure:	
Materials	158,000
Salaries	184,000
Other expenditure	72,000
Total	414,000

8 Year 2 Income and expenditure (projected).

Plot structure

The case outlines the progress of a small home security business during its first two years of trading. At the end of this period the business is faced with the possible loss of its major customer. There are undertones of unethical business behaviour that need to be addressed.

Time structure

Straight chronological development over three-year period.

Expository structure

A key feature of the expository structure of a case is the extent to which significant events are made quite explicit, or instead are understated so that students must discover what is significant for themselves. Decisions on this will depend upon the case writer's assumptions about the experience and maturity of the student group for whom the case is written. The expository structure chosen for Holmesafe Ltd is outlined below.

In paragraph 2 students learn of Holmes's assessment of Jackson and Thomas. This is included since it is likely to colour Holmes's interpretation of his conversation with Jackson at the end of the case, and his response to it.

In paragraph 3 Jackson's assistance to Holmes is described. Here Holmes's indebtedness to Jackson is indicated but not emphasised.

In paragraph 4 Holmesafe's gift of a case of whisky to Jackson is noted but there are no value judgements made on the wisdom or ethics of this.

Paragraph 5 flags up Tables 1 and 2, which show the actual and projected income and expenditure of the business in years one and two, respectively. (Some students fail to note the difference between actual and projected, but derive learning from this oversight during discussion of the case.)

The conversation between Holmes and Jackson, reported in paragraph 6, takes place 'about mid-way through the second year'. This date is not emphasised and students may not regard it as important. For perceptive students its significance becomes apparent when they begin to assess the possible impact on year two figures if business with Dawsons is lost. Some students assume that all of year two's business will be lost whereas half the year has already passed.

Tables 1 and 2 provide data from which students can undertake some basic financial analysis, but about which some assumptions must also be made. Students can be questioned about the assumptions they make and asked to defend them. Some financial analysis could have been included within the case. However, one of the objectives for the case was that students should undertake the financial analysis for themselves, and use the results (in part) to decide what action they would take following Jackson's phone call if they were in Holmes's shoes.

Before moving on to Section 2.6, you may find it helpful to work through Exercise 3 at the end of this guide. This provides opportunities to use the McNair framework in editing a short sample case.

Editing the case draft

Pruning

We need constantly to remind ourselves of our intended audience. Is the case too easy or too difficult for them? Look back again at the case difficulty matrix discussed in Section 1.9 as you think this through.

In writing a case study there is a great temptation to try to include all the data that has been collected. Time and effort have been invested in its collection and we are reluctant to discard it. However, we need to be ruthless in this respect. It is not unusual for an established case writer to abandon half the data collected. Many cases are far too long and thereby less appealing to students. Every paragraph should be examined for the contribution it makes to the case.

The case writer should not intrude into the case since this reminds the reader that he or she is reading a case study. As a result the 'suspension of disbelief' that we are attempting to foster may be inhibited. So it is best to avoid statements such as *'The case writer interviewed several members of the management team to compare their views on the company's proposals'*.

Facts and opinions

Newcomers to case writing are sometimes preoccupied with getting the facts of a situation into the case. Frequently, however, the facts of a situation are unclear and may be disputed. Opinions can be more important than facts. Opinions give meaning to facts. They also bring a case to life. So incorporate opinions within the case, but make it clear whose opinions they are. Avoid the inclusion of your own opinions. Let case events, and the opinions of those involved, speak for themselves.

Case opening

The situation reported in a case is part of a bigger ongoing reality. So the case writer has the problem of deciding where and how to 'break into' this reality. What will be the most effective point of entry to the story in order to achieve the orientation and focus needed for the learning objectives we have in mind? These are factors that will influence the choices we make in framing the first few paragraphs. But perhaps the most important job that has to be done at the outset is to capture the reader's interest. The aim in the first sentence should be to entice the student to read on.

Common types of case opening are illustrated below.

Case openings

1 A person working on a problem or assignment, often under time pressure.

Kate Burrows had some strong criticisms to make of Techaid's management and wondered how best to present these in her report to the directors the following morning.

2 An event that implies someone will have to do something.

The telephone rang.

3 Statements of fact:

   (a) A broad statement of fact which by itself does not suggest the need for reaction but arouses the reader's interest.

      In 1992 Mainstream Software became market leader in specialist software for the footwear manufacturing industry.

   (b) A more specific statement about a company's operations.

      Orbis Ltd distributed its products nationwide through twelve exclusive wholesalers.

   (c) A very specific statement of fact which has no apparent bearing on an organisation's problems.

      It was 8.30a.m. precisely as Andrew Philips, South Midshire District Council's Director of Leisure Services, pulled his car into a vacant space in the town hall car park.

4 A provocative statement by an individual involved in the case situation.

'I wouldn't trade places with anyone else in the whole world; I have everything I have ever wanted.'

Polishing the case

This is essentially a process of reading through the case several times; tweaking a word here, changing the sequence a little, checking the grammar and vocabulary. Gifted writers may transfer their thoughts effortlessly to paper. For many of us, however, the process may be slow and irksome. Finding the right word or phrase and avoiding run-of-the-mill pitfalls are ongoing problems. Some common obstacles are listed below.

Traps for the unwary case writer

1   Jargon

     *He had an **Oedipus complex**.*

2   Acronyms

     *As a medium, her **ESP** was put to good use.*

3   Misplaced expressions

     *I hope I have enough compassion to avoid making people redundant **if necessary**.*

4   Abstract nouns

     *The public lacks an **understanding** of the **inevitability** of **exhaustion** of North Sea oil.*

5   Strings of nouns

     *The article examines **government property tax reform proposals**.*

6   Strings of prepositional phrases

     *She had read **of** the achievements **of** the Irish **of** the southern regions **of** New England.*

7   Subordinated clauses

*If universities admit all students **who** apply, they will admit many **who** are not capable of studying at university level, **which** will force them to withdraw when they find they cannot cope, **which** will be a waste of taxpayers' money.*

8   Missing links

*They want to raise the voting age to 21 **because of immaturity**.*

9   Postponed verbs

*Pressure to prevent the building of nuclear power stations and even to close existing power stations **is increasing**.*

10   Passives

*Your questions **will be answered** by my secretary.*

11   Superfluous words

*She was unable to buy a ticket at student rates **because of the fact** that she was not carrying her student union card.*

12   Less familiar words

*The customer service manager **initiated immediate** action in her endeavour to **placate** the customer.*

13   Writing about writing

The case writer will begin by discussing...

14   Negatives

> He knew that **unless** he **failed** to apply within three months compensation would **not** be **denied** to him.

Source: Greenbaum and Whitcut (1988).

The case polishing process can be assisted by getting others to read the case and comment on it. Faculty colleagues may provide helpful advice but it is equally important to obtain less 'expert' feedback. People with similar background and experience to that of the student group for whom the case was written can be particularly helpful in this respect. They can be asked to say what they saw as the main issues in the case and whether they found it interesting and readable.

Case enhancement

The focus in this guide has been upon the conventional written case. But as we work a case draft into its finished form there are ample opportunities to improve presentation through the use of graphics and colour. Tables, charts, figures, cartoons and photographs can convey information to students more effectively and attractively than pages of unbroken text.

Today's students have higher expectations than their predecessors in this respect, and multimedia approaches are increasingly adopted to present learning materials to students in more appealing ways.

Case studies on audio or video cassettes are already quite widely used, and as costs fall interactive learning using CD-ROM or the Internet is becoming more widely available. Instead of conventional written cases some teachers are now providing their students with a basic written outline which is supplemented by providing easy guided access to relevant web sites where up to date information on the subject organisation or industry can be found. In this way the student is made aware of the current and ongoing changes affecting the subject organisation, in contrast to the inevitably dated events that are recorded in a written case.

However, we need to be sure as teachers that new approaches are as effective as they are fashionable. We need to think about the criteria we might use in evaluating the effectiveness of different media. Costs are clearly important – how much learning per student does the medium deliver for each £1 we spend on it? But we might also wish to include among our criteria such factors as responsiveness, flexibility, accessibility and reliability. A student group with a case and a good case teacher, it seems to me, still has a lot going for it – even if in future, they are not necessarily all at the same physical location!

Calling a halt

Knowing when to stop polishing a case may not be easy. Even the most successful of writers struggle to express what they really want to say. Author Malcolm Bradbury is said to rewrite every paragraph up to ten times before he is satisfied. Five versions of a chapter opening from his novel, *The History Man*, are shown in Appendix 3. Which one would you have used?

Setting the case aside for a while can be helpful. If when we return to it again, and it seems to read well, the narrative flowing smoothly with no obvious glitches, then we can probably call it a day and try it out in class. If all goes well we can turn our attention to preparing a teaching note for the case. This is discussed in the following section.

The case teaching note

A teaching note serves two main purposes. Primarily it provides information helpful to other users of the case, by summarising the learning objectives the case writer had in mind, salient issues within the case and the writer's experiences in using the case with students. Prospective users, too, find teaching notes helpful in searching for new cases for their courses.

A teaching note can also be useful at the writing stage by providing a framework for structuring the case and guiding the data collection process.

To some extent writing a case teaching note is an altruistic act on the part of the author, but not entirely so. Publishers of case collections may require authors to provide teaching notes. The ECCH strongly encourages case writers to do so. And if we want our cases to be used by others there is a strong incentive to write a teaching note for them.

The facts speak for themselves. Of ECCH's total collection of some 15,000 cases only about 25% have teaching notes. However, for the 50 most popular cases this figure rises to more than 80%.

Although the teaching note is of value primarily to potential users, it is not without benefits to the case author. Some case writers find it very helpful to draft an outline of a teaching note *before* teaching a case for the first time. This can help to clarify and structure thinking about *what* the case session is intended to achieve and *how* this might be brought about.

Of course this draft will need to be *revised in the light of experience* of actually using the case with students, but preparing an initial pre-teaching draft can still be very useful.

The content of teaching notes varies considerably, but it should include as *a minimum*, the key elements shown below.

The case teaching note: Key elements

1   Summary of the case

2   Teaching objectives and target audience

3   Teaching approach and strategy

4   Analysis

5   Additional readings or references

In deciding what to include in a teaching note it can be helpful to think through the following questions:

> To help me **select a suitable case** what should a teaching note include?

> To help me **maximise student learning** from cases what should a teaching note include?

You may also find it helpful to reflect on the tasks of the case teacher, summarised in Appendix 5, and to consider what assistance the teaching note might offer for each of these. An example of a teaching note, for the Holmesafe Ltd case study, is shown in Appendix 4.

An outline structure for teaching notes is shown below, which indicates most of the information sought by prospective users of a case.

Outline for case teaching notes

1   Synopsis of the case

    Provides a brief description of what the case is about, and the context in which it is set.

2   Course use

    Indicates the target learning group for whom the case was written, or with whom it has been used.

3   Teaching objectives and key issues

    Sets out, perhaps with specific behavioural objectives, the intended learning outcomes, and identifies key issues within the case that are helpful in bringing these about.

4   Teaching strategy

    Describes how the case may be used in class. It may suggest trigger questions with which to open the case discussion, suggestions for group work with the case, how to consolidate learning at the end of the case session, and so on. This section will generally reflect the case writer's own teaching style.

5   Questions for discussion

A list of questions designed to promote discussion of the key issues within the case.

6   Analysis of data

Where the case contains quantitative data for analysis it can be helpful to other users if the results of essential 'number crunching' are provide in the teaching note. This can provide a useful check against which the teacher's own calculations can be compared.

7   Background reading

This may provide references to relevant supplementary material on the case or related issues. It may also provide information on 'what happened' in the case situation, which is something students are usually keen to know.

8   Experience of using the case

Feedback on how the case has worked in different classes, and the range of case issues on which students have tended to focus, can be useful to know when preparing for a teaching session with the case.

Case release

Field researched cases

Before a case based on field research can be used for teaching or examination purposes, permission for such use must be given by the subject organisation, i.e. case release must be obtained. This is normally obtained by asking the organisation to sign a form or letter authorising its use.

Normally this will be the culmination of continuing dialogue with the host organisation during data collection and case drafting stages. During this period the question of what the organisation will or will not allow to appear in the final case should be checked out on a regular basis so that final release becomes a matter of routine rather than a source of difficulty.

The release of a case may be requested by sending two copies of a letter, or form, that includes something along the following lines.

> **Extract from a case release request**
>
> I very much appreciate your cooperation over the past few weeks in allowing me to talk to you and your staff about the restructuring you have recently implemented within the company. On the basis of these discussions and the documents you kindly provided, we have prepared the attached case study entitled '................'. I hope this reflects the key issues that you had to address without revealing any confidential information. We believe the case will make a valuable contribution to the teaching of ... on our courses.
>
> When you have noted any final corrections you wish me to make will you please sign and return one copy of this letter to indicate your agreement to publication of the case and its distribution by the European Case Clearing House for educational use.
>
> Signed:
>
> Position:
>
> Date:

Once the signed copy of the letter is returned from the subject organisation the distribution and classroom use of the case can begin.

If a case is used without such release it places the case writer and his or her employer at risk. Unauthorised use of a case could lead to a claim for damages arising from divulgence of commercially sensitive information. At the very least the willingness of organisations to cooperate with the teaching institution in future research is likely to be severely compromised. In short, 'don't use unless released'.

Apart from formal release of the case it is customary to add a footnote to page one acknowledging the cooperation of the subject organisation and commenting on the intended use of the case. An example is shown below.

> *This case was made possible through the generous cooperation of XYZ Ltd. The case is intended as a basis for class discussion rather than to illustrate either effective or ineffective handling of management situations.*
>
> *© AN Other, 199X*

Desk researched cases

The release of cases prepared from press reports and journal articles presents a rather different problem. If you have drawn extensively on a particular report then permission should be obtained from the publisher for use of the material within the case.

If on the other hand you have read widely on a particular topic or organisation, and then written the case on the basis of your own distillation of this, then formal release may not be necessary. However, the sources of information should be acknowledged and it may be wise to send a copy of the draft case to the subject organisation. This can be accompanied by a letter explaining your wish to use the case for teaching purposes, and your willingness to correct any errors of facts they draw to your attention. This should be done as a matter of courtesy, and can even be fruitful in gaining useful additional data for inclusion in the case.

If you have drawn extensively on a company's Offer for Sale document then, although this may be regarded as in the public domain, it is advisable to seek permission to use it. A sample letter for this purpose is shown in the box below, and is usually well received. This can be readily adapted to your own requirements.

If you are in any doubt about the legal position regarding case release it would be wise to seek further advice within your institution regarding its policy on these matters.

Sample letter

Dear (address to CEO/MD by name)*

I am responsible at ABC University for the teaching of ... on our ... course(s) and am currently updating the case materials we use on these programmes.

The growth and development of XYZ company has generated considerable admiration and press comment in recent years and so our students are familiar with the company both as course members and in many cases as customers. Thus it is a company to which they can readily relate regardless of their individual backgrounds.

Consequently I should like to include material on XYZ among the case studies we use on these courses.

The Offer for Sale document of (...date) provides much interesting information on company philosophy, structure and operational matters. I have drawn on this, and relevant press reports, in preparing the enclosed draft case study and I am writing to seek your permisson for the case to be used for teaching purposes in the University. Due acknowledgement to its source would, of course, be made.

I should be most grateful for your agreement to this request and look forward with interest to your reply.

Yours etc.

* Always seek permission at top level. Even though the CEO is unlikely to deal with the request in person, if he or she is in agreement they will pass it on to a subordinate for action, who will then find it difficult to ignore.

Exercises

U sing news items

(a) Select a news item or journal article in your own area of interest and consider how you might restructure this in order to shape it into a teaching or examination case.

To what target student group might it be directed? For what learning or assessment purpose might it be suitable? What might you need to modify, delete or add to the case in order to make it more suitable for the purpose you have chosen?

(b) Redraft the article to incorporate your ideas.

NB: This exercise lends itself to group work in which part (a) is discussed within the group and part (b) is undertaken individually.

The 'cases' produced may then be copied to each group member and a final discussion held to compare and contrast the different approaches used.

Among the points that can be discussed are whether the case has been made interesting to, and readable by, the target student group; how implicitly or explicitly the main issues have been presented; and what questions students might be asked about the case.

A question of authority

Read the following short case and consider the questions shown below.

A QUESTION OF AUTHORITY

Sean Collins, a young supervisor recently appointed to the position, reported to a middle-aged superior who had held his position for many years. He told Collins that he wanted to work him into his position gradually, and from time to time he intended vesting him with more and more authority.

However, in actual practice he made Collins consult with him over almost every aspect of his duties. Collins felt that he owed his superior respect for his experience, but was unable to carry out his job because of the time he spent with him in discussing all the details. Collins' subordinates started to think he was superfluous.

---

1   For what purposes and target student group might this make a useful case?

2   How would you improve the case opening? Suggest an alternative opening paragraph for the case.

3   Does the case title give some useful guidance to the reader about the central issue, or should a neutral, non-directive title be used instead?

4   Suggest two or three questions with which you might open a class discussion on the case.

Mallards Department Store

Read the following short case and consider the questions shown below.

MALLARDS DEPARTMENT STORE

Mallards Department Store was one of a group of three such stores located in nearby towns. All the stores were large ones. The hardware department of the Mallards store was managed by Mr R. Gudgeon, a long-serving member of the organisation. His department included normal hardware plus paints, wallpapers and a small 'do-it-yourself' section. He had two senior male assistants – the more senior of the two being a long-serving employee of the organisation, shortly due for retirement. The second of the two, Norman Twist, was appointed to succeed to the post of Senior Assistant. It had been noticeable, however, that since his appointment he had shown particular interest in the DIY section and had frequently made suggestions to Mr Gudgeon about the expansion of the section. Mr Gudgeon however, had tended to recite company policy that DIY was to be part of hardware since no great expansion was envisaged – owing partly to limitations of space on the floor occupied by hardware and partly to an assumed inability to compete with the specialist DIY shops in the town.

One morning Mr Gudgeon was summoned to the store Director's office and asked to read a report that Norman Twist had prepared, a report unbeknown to and unauthorised by anyone in the store. This had been sent directly to the store Director.

The report was a most able appraisal of the whole situation regarding DIY and particularly the position of Mallards in this field. It argued a strong case for expansion in this field and was justified by information on the market, potential competitors in the town, forecast sales, costs and profits, which despite necessary checking, showed that Twist had done his homework very thoroughly. In addition, suggestions were included regarding the reorganisation of selling space to accommodate this expansion. The biggest change, however, as far as Mr Gudgeon was concerned, was that Twist proposed a completely separate department to include DIY in its widest sense.

Mr Gudgeon had a substantial minimum salary but earned commission above this on his departmental profits. Last year the DIY section, despite its small size, earned 20% of his profits. It seemed to Mr Gudgeon that the store Director was sold on the idea and he was aware that his own stock had fallen somewhat, particularly since Twist had specified in his report the suggestions he had previously put forward to Gudgeon and the reasons they were turned down. To be fair, however, quite a number of recommendations were implemented by Gudgeon and these Twist did not mention in the report.

---

1   For what target student group(s) might this be a suitable teaching or examination case?

2   Consider the structure of the case in terms of

McNair's framework – narrative, time, plot and exposition. What suggestions do you have for improvements in respect of each of these structures?

3   How would you rate the case in terms of the case difficulty matrix discussed in Section 1.9?

4   What additional information would you wish to include in the case, and why?

5   How would you improve the case opening? Suggest an alternative opening paragraph for the case.

6   Suggest two or three questions with which you might open a class discussion on the case.

all Nurseries

Introduction

The data given below was obtained by a case researcher from conversations with an acquaintance who was about to take up an appointment as manager of Hall Nurseries, a horticultural business recently acquired by her employers.

The exercise is in two parts involving firstly small group discussion and then elements of case drafting on an individual basis. As you work through the exercise keep in mind the notion of case difficulty and also the need to combine narrative, time, plot and expository structures within a case, as discussed in Section 2.5.

Data for Hall Nurseries case

Hall Nurseries was an old established horticultural business located on a busy trunk road between a major city, 16 miles distant, and a 'new' town 4 miles to the north.

Sixty per cent of its output, mainly bedding plants, cut flowers and house plants, were sold by auction at the city flower market, and the remainder to retail and wholesale florists, who collected their requirements direct from the nurseries.

The business was a third-generation family firm, widely respected in the trade for its quality produce. However, with an ageing owner, turnover had been static for the past few years, and the business was barely profitable.

The nurseries had now been acquired by a large progressively managed fruit and vegetable producer, which supplies retail chains throughout the region and wished to extend its activities into the buoyant house plant market. The parent company's operations are centred about 25 miles NW of Hall Nurseries.

Your respondent has been asked to take over as manager of Hall Nurseries, and will report to the parent company board. Among the points noted during her initial survey of the business were the following:

1   In common with many horticultural businesses, Hall Nurseries was a management backwater. The business has been run entirely by the owner, with the assistance of a working foreman and a bookkeeper-clerk. Accounting has been confined to historical information only.

2   Total staff of 32, the majority of whom have been with the business all their working lives. Their average age is 54, and their specialist skills are an important asset of the business. Recruitment is difficult due to traditional low wages in the industry and the attractions of factory work in the new town.

3   Of the 28 hectares of freehold land, only about two thirds is under cultivation. During the past

five years two applications for planning permission to build houses on the unused land have been refused. This land is quite suitable for horticultural purposes.

4   Approximately one hectare of glass houses (at present under-utilised), barns, sheds, tractor etc. are in a reasonable state of repair.

5   Virtually all sales are made during the period March–October, with a further up-turn in December.

6   Produce collected by florists is frequently paid for in cash at the time. The previous owner has intimated that he did not always enter these cash purchases in the books, especially those to casual purchasers.

Questions and tasks

Groups

Please discuss the following questions in your group:

1   For what target audience and learning objectives might this data provide a useful case? Formulate some explicit learning outcomes that you would aim to achieve during a class discussion of the finished case.

2   What 'facts' will you make explicit within the case? What 'facts' will you incorporate in such a way that students must do a little work in order to 'discover' them?

3   Should all the material obtained in the initial 'data trawl' be incorporated in the case, or is some of this irrelevant? What additional information do you think is (a) essential and (b) desirable to include within the case?

Individuals

After you have discussed the case data in groups you are invited, on an individual basis, to:

1   Produce an outline for the case, with a brief description of the content of each section.

2   Write an opening paragraph for the case.

3   Write a concluding paragraph for the case.

4   Draft two or three questions with which you would open a class discussion on the case.

Case drafting: Geoff Brown

Introduction

The following data was obtained from discussion with Geoff Brown, a part-time tutor for a university-linked distance learning course. It concerns an incident that arose between himself and one of his students.

Data for Geoff Brown case

Background

The respondent works for a pharmaceutical company as its production manager. The incident occurred early in his second year as a part-time tutor for the university. He had become a tutor at the invitation of the university's regional manager. She had met the respondent through his involvement in his company's internal manager development programme, which incorporated her university's learning materials.

Tutor's job

1   To run six half-day tutorials for a group of students in his area, during the one-year course.

2 To mark four assessed assignments during the year.

3 To provide telephone support to individual members of the group on request.

Sequence of events surrounding the incident

1 Tutor marked the first assessed assignment and returned these to students.

2 Tutor received phone call from an angry student who complained about what he considered a low mark. The student called the mark of 40% derisory and claimed that he had never previously received a mark of less than 60%. He complained of 'inadequate written feedback' from the tutor on his assignment. He said that comments such as 'Can you explain this more fully?', 'What other examples can you suggest?', 'Have you considered other alternatives?' were vague and unhelpful and that had he responded to these he would have exceeded the word limit for the assignment.

3 The tutor asked the student to return the assignment to him and said he would look at it again to see if he could find a few more marks.

4 The tutor increased his mark to 48%.

5 The student still felt this was too low, but took the matter no further. Relations between the tutor and student remained cool for the remainder of the course.

Discussion between case researcher and tutor

The tutor said he had found it very difficult not to respond to the student's angry telephone call in similar terms. He quickly realised the possible implications of his agreeing to say he would try to find the student a few more marks. He did not want to earn the reputation among students that his marks were open to challenge or that he was flexible in his marking.

He considered asking another tutor to mark the assignment in question, but decided against this on two counts. He did not want to add to colleagues' already considerable marking workload. Also, he did not want to admit a lack of confidence in his own judgement.

The incident made him reflect on the subjectivity of the assignment marking process, and the difficulty of communicating to students the distinction between good and poor assignments.

If the student remained unsatisfied and began a formal appeal this would involve considerable unpleasant hassle, and if the appeal was successful the tutor wondered how this would affect his credibility and future relationships with his students and the institution. He admitted, with regret, that this had been a factor in his decision to increase the student's mark.

The tutor wondered what he might have done to have prevented the incident. How could he convince students of the fairness of his marking when there was an inevitable element of subjectivity involved in marking a case analysis?

Additional data collected by case researcher

The course

Course materials comprised a course text, a series of study booklets and a set of case studies. Case studies featured strongly in the course and were used for ongoing assessment, tutorials and in the final examination. The tutor had no discretion in the choice of case studies, either for the assessed assignments or for the tutorials, as these were mailed to staff and students from the university at the start of the course. Students' individual home studies were supplemented by six Saturday morning group tutorials spread through the academic year.

Assessment

This was based on four assessed assignments submitted during the year and an end of course examination. Assessed assignments and examinations were weighted equally. To obtain a diploma students had to achieve an overall average mark of 50% or more, and a minimum of 40% in the examination and an average of 40% or more for the assessed assignments.

Assessed assignments were based on case studies. In marking these tutors used a marking scheme in which 50% of available marks were allocated to the application of course concepts in the analysis of the case, 30% for arguments and conclusions and 20% for structure, organisation and overall cohesiveness. For each assessed assignment tutors were also provided with a broad indication of the characteristics of excellent, middle range, borderline and fail grade assignments. However, these were rather subjective but as there were seldom 'right answers' to a case study this was regarded as inevitable.

Marked assignments were sent by tutors to the university where they were recorded, sampled for consistency of marking, and then returned to students. During his first year the tutor received periodic feedback from the university on how his marks compared with those of other tutors. This showed that he was a little more generous than other tutors but not significantly so. Examinations were set and marked centrally by staff at the university.

Conclusion

The respondent agreed that the data could be written up as a case study, but only if all names were changed.

Questions and tasks

1   For what target audience and learning objectives might the Geoff Brown data provide a useful case? Formulate some explicit learning outcomes that you would aim to achieve during a class discussion of the finished case.

2   When you have answered question 1, you are invited to work up the data into a teaching case.

You will need to decide what type of case you will write from this data. Should it be a conventional problem-orientated case study written as a single document? Does the data lend itself to presentation in several sequential episodes? What might be the advantages of the latter method of presentation?

Once you have decided on the type of case to write, prepare an outline for it of the type described in Section 2.4. From this outline you can then begin to flesh out the details of the case.

It is often best to begin working on the middle section of the case rather than worry about the opening paragraph at this stage in the process.

As you consider how to introduce the main case issues keep in mind the notion of case difficulty and also the need to combine narrative, time, plot and expository structures within a case, as discussed in Section 2.5. What 'facts' will you make explicit within the case? What 'facts' will you incorporate in such a way that students must do a little work in order to 'discover' them?

Some case writers prepare an outline teaching note as they draft a case. They find this helps them to structure the case so that it better meets their teaching needs. You might find it helpful to work in this way. Think about how you will open a class discussion on the case, and draft two or three questions for this purpose in your teaching note.

Once you are reasonably satisfied with the main body of the case, the opening and closing paragraphs can be considered. These need to be thought about very carefully, the former in particular. It has an important job to do in capturing the reader's interest. Some examples of difference case openings were given in Section 2.6.

When you have finished a draft of the case ask someone to read it and give you some comments on it. If the reader is someone with a similar background and experience to your target audience, so much the better. A teaching colleague can be asked to give you some feedback on the draft from a tutor's perspective.

Case drafting: Meadows Machinery plc

Introduction

A competitor of Meadows Machinery plc has recently launched a machine that appears to be superior to the equivalent Meadows product. Data about this situation has been collected and is given below. Read this data and then tackle the questions and tasks that follow.

Data for Meadows Machinery case study

Background information on Meadows

Leading supplier of filling and sealing machines. These are sold to both the chemical industry (approximately 40% market share) and the food industry (approximately 30% market share). Estimated installed base of Meadows machines: 4,000 (chemical industry), 5,000 (food industry).

Financial information on Meadows

	£ m		£ m
Total machines sales (800 units p.a.)	40.0	Spare part sales	10.0
Matls and parts costs	9.6	Gross margin on spare parts	5.0
D. labour costs	8.0		
Other manf. costs	8.0		
Total manf. costs	25.6		
Gross profit	14.4		
Selling and admin. costs	8.0		
Net profit	6.4		

Meadows people involved

John Starling, General Manager

Director of Engineering

Sales Manager

Chairman

Competitive threat

New machine launched by a German company, A. Stiel, for the chemical industry. Incorporates critical components made of a new composite material. Meadows machines use a special alloy steel for these parts, which they purchase under an exclusive contract. Stiel claims their new machine runs at higher operating speeds and has a longer life than equivalent Meadows machine. It has been aggressively priced at 20% below the selling price of the Meadows machine. No other information available on A. Stiel at this stage. Need to investigate further? Seek information from Meadows, library research?

Meadows stock situation

Special steel units: 92 units costed at £192,000. This is sufficient for approximately six weeks production at current rates if used in both chemical and food industry machines. Special steel: sufficient for 180 units, costed at £288,000 (i.e. £1,600 per unit). This is sufficient for approximately eleven weeks production at current rates. Cost of new composite parts for Meadows machines is estimated at 40% of existing special steel units.

Issues and options discussed by people involved

Scale of threat posed by competitor's move and how best to respond. Option of replicating features provided by competitor's machine. This is advocated by sales manager as soon as possible – estimated to take two months. Option of redesigning entire chemical line to incorporate competitor features and include other improvements – suggested by general manager – time horizon less certain. Likely consequences of various options on sales revenue, costs, profits, market standing, etc.

Questions and tasks

1   For what target audience and learning objectives might this data provide a useful case? Formulate some explicit learning outcomes that you would aim to achieve during a class discussion of the finished case.

2   What 'facts' will you make explicit within the case? What 'facts' will you incorporate in such a way that students must do a little work in order to 'discover' them?

3   Should all the material obtained in the initial 'data trawl' be incorporated in the case or is some of this irrelevant? What additional information do you think is (a) essential and (b) desirable to include within the case?

4   Produce an outline for the case, with a brief description of the content of each section.

5   Write an opening paragraph for the case.

6   Write a concluding paragraph for the case.

7   Draft two or three questions with which you would open a class discussion on the case.

Appendices

Case research preparation

Intended case

1 What type of case do you intend to write? (see Section 1.3)

  (a) Incident case(s)

  (b) Background case

  (c) Exercise case

  (d) Situation case

  (e) Complex case

  (f) Decision case

2 What are the main issues (three or four) that you want the case to raise?

  ....

  ....

  ....

  ....

  ....

  ....

3 What teaching/learning objectives do you have in mind? What learning do you want to bring about with the case? What do you want students to:

know ....

and/or

be able to do (or do better) ....

and/or

have formed an opinion about ....

as a result of working on the case?

Participating organisation

4 Has contact been made with the subject organisation? If yes, at what level?

....

5 Does this person know what a case study is and how it is likely to be used for teaching purposes?

....

6 Does your contact have authority to approve and release the finished case for teaching purposes?

....

7 Is your contact clear about the precise nature of the cooperation you are seeking? Has the organisation agreed to cooperate on this basis?

....

Data collection

8 Have you decided what data you wish to collect for the case?

....

....

9 Can some of this be collected from published sources to minimise the direct demands you will make on the subject organisation?

....

....

10 How do you propose collecting the data you need from within the subject organisation?

    (a) Questionnaire?

    (b) Interviews? (recorded?)

    (c) Direct observation?

    (d) Perusal (or photocopies) of internal documents?

    (e) Other?

11 Is the subject organisation agreeable to your collecting data in these ways?

....

12 Have you considered how you will introduce yourself, and the purpose of your case research, to your various respondents within the organisation?

....

Cases on small businesses: Writer's brief

Aim

To produce several case studies on the management of small businesses during their formation and first few years of operation.

Areas of interest

The cases should allow students to consider the issues detailed in the following subsections.

Motivation

What prompted the owner(s) to set up in business? What were their objectives in doing so?

Personality and background

What kind of people are the owner(s)? What personality traits are evident? For example, are they energetic, creative, extrovert, etc? What are their ages, family background, education, qualifications, business experience and leisure interests? What particular strengths do they believe they possess? What weaknesses, if any, do they acknowledge? What do other people think? What are their values, for example attitude to risk, business ethics, etc.?

Sequence of events in setting up business

What were their first steps in establishing the business? How much pre-planning was done?

Problem areas

What problems were anticipated by the owner(s) and what did they do about minimising these? What unexpected problems did they face and how did they respond to these?

Relationships

What were and are the owners' significant relationships, for example, spouse, family, business and social contacts? To what extent were these relations utilised in establishing the business? What significant business relationships have been built up since starting the business and to what extent have these also become important social relationships?

Management of the business

The business proposition. Did the owners perceive a clear business opportunity from the outset? Is there evidence of analysis and planning, for example, analysis of market potential and the resources needed in financial, human and physical terms to establish and maintain the business? What are the owners' time horizons? How, if at all, is the environment monitored for threats and opportunities? What are the basic operational activities of the business; how are these monitored and controlled and by whom?

What proportion of the owners' time is devoted to the day-to-day operations and how much to development and planning for the future? What hours do they work and how do they respond to pressure? To what extent have the owners delegated work to others? What kind of work has been delegated?

Reflection

What are the owners' views on the current position of the business? How do they see it developing in the future? What lessons have they learned to date and what would they do differently if starting again? What has given them most satisfaction and what has caused them greatest concern?

Getting it right: Malcolm Bradbury

Five different openings for a chapter in *The History Man*, by Malcolm Bradbury. *Source*: an article on writing style in the *Sunday Times* Colour Supplement. Reprinted with the permission of Curtis Brown on behalf of Malcolm Bradbury. Copyright © Malcolm Bradbury 1975.

•

In the morning Howard woke up in green and white striped pyjamas to unmitigated daylight, a busy teaching programme, and the detritus of his party. He inspected the contents of his head; a residue of pleasure, guilt and migraine was suspended there from last night. He opened his eyes and inspected the bed; it was his own. He turned and inspected his companion: it was Barbara. He turned his head and inspected the Habitat alarm clock on the side table: the time, it said, was VII to VIII.

•

Three days later, on the Monday morning, Howard Kirk wakes up in an unhappy temper. Surfacing out of unconsciousness and into being, he finds the space in the bed beside him empty; Barbara is already up. He groans, and smoothes his hair down, and looks out of the window: a heavy rain is pouring down, washing dreariness over the damaged houses. He gets out of bed and pads along the landing to the bathroom, to sculpt round the elegance of

his Zapata moustache. He plugs his razor into the two little holes beneath the bleak round globe of the light. His
face comes up in the mirror; in the cool urban sheen of
the morning he inspects the Condition of Man. It is
unpromising.

•

On Monday morning, with the weekend over, the life
of ordinary things returns to the Kirks. Howard has classes that morning; Barbara goes to Sainsbury's; the children
go to school. The noise begins soon after seven, a laughing, a bellowing, a crying from the children's rooms.
Barbara gets up, and puts on the Biba housecoat; Howard
tries to deaden, for a little longer, the sounds that bring
him towards consciousness. The bed bounces as Barbara
gets out; the lavatory flushes several times; the noise
recedes downstairs. Howard gets out of bed and pads
along the landing to the bathroom, plugs his razor into the
two black holes beneath the bleak globe of the light, and
pulls the cord. His face comes up in the mirror; in the cool
urban sheen of the morning he inspects the Condition of
Man.

•

On the Monday morning, with the weekend over, the
Kirks always wake early. Monday is a busy day for the
Kirks: Howard has his classes, and the week's teaching to
plan; there are children to be got to school; Barbara, with
a couple of partners in the Progressive Shoppers' group,
always goes to the grocery wholesalers that morning for a
bulk purchase which she then has to distribute: tinned
fruit, cereals, cooking oil, baked beans, lavatory paper to
be split up and circulated. They wake up early, already

stirred by the heavy noise of traffic on the urban motor-way, the buzz of motor-scooters on the streets nearby. A laughing, a bellowing, a crying from the children's room. Barbara gets up first; the bed bounces as she rises, pads to the door, puts on the Biba housecoat. In the big bed, under the Madras bedspread, Howard rests a little longer.

•

It is four in the morning when the party comes to its end. The Kirks, that hospitable couple, usher them forth, and then they go upstairs to their disorderly bedroom, which smells sharply of pot, and push the bed back into position, and take the ashtrays off it, and undress, and get under the duvet. They say nothing, being tired people; they do not touch each other, having no need; Barbara, in her black night-dress, folds her body into Howard's, her buttocks on his knees, and they are quickly asleep. And then it is the morning, and the Habitat alarm clock rings on the bedside table, and they wake again, back into the life of ordinary things. Consciousness returns and feels heavy with use; Howard presses his eyelids open, jerks towards being, regresses again. The bed vibrates and bounces; Barbara is getting up. The Habitat alarm clock says it is V to VIII.

Holmesafe Ltd: Teaching note

1 Summary of the case

This two-page case outlines the progress of a small home security business during its first two years of trading. At the end of this period the business is faced with the possible loss of its major customer. There are undertones of unethical business behaviour that need to be addressed.

2 Teaching objectives and target audience

(a) Teaching objectives

At the end of the case analysis and discussion, students should be more aware that business managers and proprietors need to address not only objective quantifiable issues, but also less tangible, ethical dilemmas. For a new, developing business, decisions taken on ethical issues help to shape the values and culture of the organisation.

(b) Target audience

The case has been used on a variety of small business management courses. It has also been used in the early stages of strategic management courses at DMS and MBA levels.

3 Teaching approach and strategy

An approach that works well is to begin with a conventional analysis of the recent performance and present position of the business before moving on to consider the more problematic ethical issues.

Students are given no specific assignments before class other than to read the case and consider the issues it raises. A useful, general question with which to begin the class discussion is:

How well has Holmesafe performed to date?

This invites students to examine the performance of Holmesafe in terms of profitability and growth. It may also be used to trigger a more general discussion of business performance criteria and their relevance to a newly established business.

The discussion may then be switched to consideration of Holmesafe's position at the end of the case with a question such as:

*How well placed do you think Holmesafe is to face
the future?*

This discussion can be usefully structured around the strengths, weaknesses, opportunities and threats Holmesafe faces. Students may already be familiar with SWOT analysis and if so will normally use this approach. If not, the framework can usefully be introduced with this case.

The possibility of losing its major customer is a serious threat and an obvious one to students. However, some students will not pick up the ethical issues implicit in Jackson's phone call to Holmes. The tutor can move the discussion on to this theme by asking a question along the lines of:

> What do you make of Jackson's phone call to Holmes?

There are several possible interpretations, and these should be noted as students offer them. These conflicting views on the phone call, and the range of responses open to Jackson as a result, are central issues in the case and its richest source of potential learning.

The nature of the dilemma faced by Holmes can be probed by asking such questions as:

> How important is the decision Holmes must make, for the future of the business?

> How big a problem is this?

> Is it an operational or policy/strategy matter?

Discussion of what action Holmes should now take can be energised by asking students:

> What would you now do if in Holmes's position?

This question can be expanded by asking them to consider immediate, short-term and longer term actions.

The closing stages of the discussion are used by the author to bring together several general issues. In summary these are:

- the risks arising from dependence on a major customer;

- the need to monitor and respond to the competitive environment;

- the culture-shaping significance of ethical decisions of the kind depicted in the case.

4 Analysis

(a) Business performance

There is only limited information within the case on which to assess business performance. A crude indication of net profit can be determined as the difference between income and expenditure, but since no balance sheets are provided neither return on capital nor working capital management can be explored. However, some analysis is possible to show, for example, the proportion of total sales accounted for by different customers and business areas, the breakdown of expenditure by category and comparisons between first year figures (actual) and those projected for year two.

The case concludes mid-way through year two, but there is no information on whether year two projections have been updated in the light of actual performance in the first half of year two. From Table 1 it can be seen that business with Dawsons accounted for over 50% of total sales in year one. Although reduced to 47.7% of projected sales in year two, Holmesafe remains highly dependent on sales to Dawsons.

Profit margins are good and show further projected improvements in year two. There is a significant projected increase in the advisory services area of the business and this should reduce the early reliance on the sale of products.

Table 1

	YEAR 1 actual	% of income	YEAR 2 projected
Income (£)			
From Dawsons	216,000	50.53	270,000
From Rowans	144,000	33.68	162,000
Other sales	54,000	12.63	71,000
Advisory services	13,500	3.16	63,000
Total income	427,500	100.00	566,000

(b) SWOT analysis

SWOT analysis of Holmesafe suggests the following:

Strengths	**Weaknesses**
Good sales growth	Undue reliance on major customer
Good profit margins	Poor marketing?
Good cash flow	Unaware of competition?
Advisory business developing strongly	Careless of relationship with Jackson
Technical innovation?	
Threats	**Opportunities**
Loss of major customer	Security a growth industry
Competition (superiority of competitor's products?)	Greater use of Holmes's inventive skill?
Relationship with Jackson	Broadening of product range
	Broadening of customer base

(c) Conversation with Jackson

A range of interpretations is possible ranging from:

> *Jackson's information is true, and there is no ulterior motive in his request for assistance in finding a part-time job.*

to:

Jackson is seeking a 'sweetener' from Holmes in return for placing Dawsons business with Holmesafe. The information about the competition from Browns may be exaggerated or untrue.

(d) Options open to Holmes

These will depend on the interpretation placed on Jackson's phone call. One option would be to probe Jackson carefully to gain a better understanding of the facts of the situation and Jackson's motives. Holmes has some days ('let's meet for lunch on Saturday to talk things over') in which to find out more about the merits of competing products. If it transpires that Jackson is seeking a bribe from Holmesafe in order to retain Dawsons's business, Holmes's response to this will depend on what he regards as acceptable and unacceptable business behaviour.

Holmes could consider going over Jackson's head directly to Thomas in order to resolve the matter (he had earlier assessed Thomas as a man of integrity). The risks of this need to be assessed carefully. It might be argued that Holmesafe has already compromised its relationship with Dawsons by the presentation to Jackson of a case of whisky at the end of year one.

(e) 'What if?' analysis

Assuming that the contract with Dawsons is lost, the remaining 50% of projected year two sales to Dawsons, amounting to £135,000 might be lost. (At this stage the business is half-way through year two so it can be assumed that 50% of the year's projected sales to

Dawsons have already been made). If these sales cannot be made up elsewhere the revised projected income for year two might be as shown in Table 2.

Table 2: Projected income and expenditure for second year

Income:		£
From Dawsons		135,000
From Rowans		162,000
Other sales		71,000
Advisory services		63,000
	Total	431,000

Expenditure:		
Materials		158,000
Salaries		184,000
Other expenditure		72,000
	Total	414,000
	Net profit	17,000

The situation should be rather better than shown in Table 2. There are likely to be savings in respect of materials and salary costs that are no longer incurred in respect of the cancelled Dawsons contract.

5 Additional reading and references

SWOT analysis is a well-established framework of strategic analysis and is featured in most texts on general management, business policy or strategic management.

Ethical issues are dealt with rather more patchily but see, for example, various articles in the *Journal of Business Ethics*.

6 Feedback

The majority of students with whom this case has been used do believe that Jackson was trying to obtain additional reward for continuing to buy from Holmesafe. They also believe that this behaviour is an occasional feature of business life and must be dealt with on the basis of the values held by the decision makers involved, as well as the law of the land.

A small percentage of students are shocked to discover that such situations arise. Some students point to similar ethical dilemmas that arise when doing business overseas in cultures that have different values from our own.

Tasks of the case teacher

1   Define educational objectives.

2   Select appropriate teaching materials.

3   Choose a starting point for the case discussion.

4   Analyse case data thoroughly before the discussion.

5   Keep the discussion focused on central themes.

6   Select transition points.

7   Manage student contributions.

8   Manage own verbal behaviour.

9   Probe student comments.

10   Manage presentations of assumptions and evidence.

11   Manage conflict around central issues.

12   Manage the blackboards / flip-charts.

13   Manage any audio-visuals.

14   Summarise the discussion.

15   Draw cross-case linkages.

16   Draw out conceptual frameworks and generalisations.

Source: Bonoma (1989).

Cases in management: A student's guide

Introduction

You may not have had previous experience of the case study method and the purpose of this note is to describe the use of case studies in management teaching, and to make some suggestions which you may find useful for preparing cases and discussing them in class.

Nature and purpose of case studies

A case study is a description of a situation that has arisen in an organisation. Most of the cases to be used in the course describe real situations, although some will fall into the category known as 'armchair' cases. Cases vary considerably in length; they may contain very little detail, or a seemingly baffling amount of detail. They may be addressed to a very specific problem or they may cover a great range of problems. Sometimes the problem for discussion is obvious, sometimes it is not. Cases rarely contain all the information that the reader would like to find. This is a criticism often levelled at the case study method, but it must be remembered that in real life one rarely has all the information one would like.

The basic purpose of case studies is to provide students of management with simulated decision making experiences. The case provides a vehicle for the analysis of problems, for the derivation of solutions to the problems and for consideration of the difficulties that would be encountered in implementing these solutions.

Cases do not have a right and wrong answer. Answers may be good or bad, but this to a great extent depends on the supporting arguments and the use that is made of available information. The lack of right and wrong answers can lead to frustration. Again, however, bear in mind that there are very few clear-cut right and wrong answers to problems in the real world.

Preparation of case studies

There is no best way of preparing a case study. Each individual will obviously develop his or her own particular approach. Many people do, however, find it helpful to prepare a case study by first reading it through quickly to gain an understanding of the overall situation and to identify the major problem areas. This can be followed by a detailed examination of the case, during which notes should be made.

These notes should detail the problems, use the available information to provide a solution, and describe the problems of solution implementation. It is important that numerical information, where provided, should be used, and where information appears to be lacking, intelligent assumptions should be made in order to arrive at solutions. Care should be taken to develop arguments with the available facts and to ensure that any assumptions made can be reasonably justified.

Discussion of case studies

One of the advantages of the case study method is that it provides an opportunity for presenting arguments to one's peer group. The effective manager is almost certainly going to have to acquire this facility. Those who find difficulty in making oral presentations in front of other people should try to overcome this during the course. The case study provides a vehicle for interaction between the course tutor and course members. It is also meant to provide interaction between course members. You are therefore encouraged to question your fellow course members' points of view so long as you have sound reasons for doing so. You may feel the case method is a somewhat cumbersome way of learning. Undoubtedly less information is passed from teacher to student than can be achieved in a straight lecture. However, much of management teaching is not about passing information from teacher to student. Information can be obtained from reading books. Classroom time can often be used to greater advantage in discussing the usefulness and practicability of information and techniques relating to the solution of managerial problems.

It is hoped that the case study method will do this successfully and make a more useful and lasting impression on course members than a series of straight lectures would do.

Case incidents: A student's guide

You may not have had previous experience of the case incident method. The purpose of this note is to describe ways in which incidents may be used on training courses, and to make some suggestions which you may find helpful in examining incidents and discussing them with your course colleagues and tutor.

Nature and purpose of case incidents

The collection of incidents for which this note was written are descriptions of situations that have occurred in organisations and with which a supervisor has been concerned. All of the incidents are real – they are not the figment of an author's imagination. They have caused concern to the people who were involved in them. They are the kinds of incidents that supervisors face every day. The incidents have not been elaborated; they are presented briefly, as they were recounted by the people involved. You may feel that they are too brief; that they contain insufficient information for a worthwhile analysis or discussion. If so, ask yourself what additional information you would like to have concerning the incident. Do you think this information would have been available to the participants in the incident? How would this additional information further your understanding of the incident, or help you towards the resolution of a problem?

Incidents provide a vehicle for the analysis of situations, for considering solutions to problems identified and the difficulties that might be encountered in implementing those solutions. They do not have right and wrong answers. Some approaches to the situations described may be better than others in certain circumstances. We can seldom be more prescriptive than this. The lack of right and wrong answers can lead to frustration. It is quite possible that your tutor may be reluctant to give you his or her own analysis of the incident. Bear in mind however, that there are very few clear-cut, right and wrong answers to problems in the real world. What is important is that you make the best use of the information available concerning the incident, listen carefully to the views of other course members, and then make up your own mind about the incident and the issues it raises.

Discussion of incidents

Discussion of incidents provides a vehicle for interaction between the course tutor and course members. It is also meant to provide interaction among course members. One of the benefits of the incident approach is that it provides an opportunity for course members to present views to others. The effective supervisor needs to develop this ability. Those who find difficulty in making oral presentations in front of other people should take the opportunity in discussing incidents to try to overcome this problem.

Get involved in the discussion. Remember that in a discussion, course members are dependent upon one another for learning. The more you participate, the more you will benefit. This is because your contributions are likely to be challenged and you will have the opportunity to defend your views in the discussion. In this way you will influence others, as well as be influenced by them.

There is frequently a temptation to dismiss some contributions too readily. Recognise that you can benefit not only from the insight and experience of your colleagues, but can also learn from their inaccurate observations and prejudices. Value their contributions; do not discard them lightly, even where they conflict with your own views. Have confidence in your own experiences. Your work experiences are valuable to your colleagues and can help them to understand what goes on in organisations. Be willing to share your experiences with the group.

Recognise that the way you look at situations and interpret them will be influenced by your values. The values you hold will also influence your choice of solutions to problems. The more you try to understand your own values through discussion, the more you will become aware of your own prejudices and preferences. In discussion, try to avoid the easy cliche, the stock response and challenge the shallow responses of your course colleagues – or tutor! Try to achieve more than a superficial analysis of the incident under discussion. Be willing to probe, and dig beneath the surface of the situation described.

Structuring your analysis

You will find it helpful to introduce structure into your analysis. For example, there will be a diagnostic phase in your discussion, in which you should examine the situation in terms of what is really going on, what is causing poor performance, what would be considered appropriate behaviour in the situation, and so on. This may be followed by an action planning phase in which decisions, or courses of action that could be taken in the situation concerned, are proposed and evaluated.

Learning through incidents

You may feel that discussing case incidents is a cumbersome way of learning. It is true that less information is passed from tutor to course member than can be achieved, for example, through a straight lecture. However, becoming an effective supervisor requires more than the acquisition of information. Information, in any case, can usually be obtained from books. Classroom time can often be used to greater advantage in discussing the usefulness and practicability of information and theories relating to the work of the supervisor.

Learning through the discussion of case incidents comes not only from the issues raised by the incident. Much can also be learned from the study of your own behaviour, and the behaviour of others, during the discussion. Who are the discussion leaders, and how does this become apparent? What are the qualities of a good negotiator? Who are good listeners? Who shows sensitivity to the feelings of others? Who encourages contributions from colleagues and how is this done? Who is able to build effectively upon the contributions of others? Who keeps the discussion going in a productive way when there is a lag in the proceedings? What would your colleagues say of *your* role in all these activities?

Thus, the incident discussion is an opportunity for you to observe, practise and develop your own interpersonal skills. We hope that you enjoy your analysis and discussion of case incidents and find it a valuable learning experience.

References and sources

p5   **The Lancaster model of learning**
Donald Binsted, from an unpublished
working paper, Management Teacher
Development Unit, University of Lancaster,
England.

p8   **Forms of learning session**
Donald D. Simmons, *Notes on the Case
Study*, The Case Clearing House of Great
Britain & Ireland (now The European Case
Clearing House), 1974.

p13   **Types of case study**
Donald D. Simmons, *op.cit.*

p51 **Case difficulty**
James A. Erskine, Michiel R. Leenders and Louise A. Mauffette-Leenders, *Teaching with Cases*, School of Business Administration, The University of Western Ontario, London, Canada, 1981.

p81 **Case structure**
Extracted from Harvard Business School note 9-372-303, Malcolm P. McNair, *McNair on cases*, Harvard Business School, Boston, Massachusetts, 1972.

p83 **Telling stories**
Stephen Clark, A very big gig, *Sunday Telegraph*, 17 November 1996.

p96 **Traps for the unwary case writer**
Sidney Greenbaum and Janet Whitcut, *Longman Guide to English Usage*, Longman, Harlow, 1988.

p159 **Appendix 5**
Extracted from Harvard Business School note 9-589-083, Thomas V. Bonoma, *Hints for writing teaching notes*, Harvard Business School, Boston, Massachusetts, 1989.

p161   **Appendix 6**
Cranfield School of Management
As issued to MBA students in 1971.

p165   **Appendix 7**
Adapted from Appendix 6 to suit incidents
rather than cases (see above).

Index

analysis, xi, xii, 11, 12, 14, 22, 27, 30, 31, 36, 50, 51–52, 56, 92, 102, 104, 127, 128, 142, 149, 150, 152–157, 161, 165, 166, 167–168 *(see also SWOT analysis, written analysis)*
armchair cases, 62, 69–71
assessment, 18, 55, 56, 91, 113, 128
assumptions, 12, 39, 91, 92, 159, 162
awkward incident case, 35–40
    discussion of, 36–40 *(see also discussion)*

beliefs about how people learn, 9
briefing, research assistants, 68, 141–143

case
    development, xii, 61–62
    draft, 73–80, 93–100
    enhancement, 61, 98–99
    incidents, 13, 35–40, 41, 165–168 *(see also incidents)*
    release, 67, 70, 105–109
    structure of, 70, 81–92, 118 *(see also structure)*
    types of, 13–15, 68

case method, ix, xii, 11–12, 13, 16, 21, 46, 47, 161, 163
  classic, 11
  complaints about, 45
case study, definition of, xi, 161
case teaching note, 101–104 *(see also Holmesafe case, teaching note; teaching note)*
concepts, 4, 51, 52, 128
course member(s), 11, 15, 17, 18, 19, 36, 37, 39, 40, 45, 109, 163, 166, 168

data
  collection, 36, 61, 68, 101, 105, 139
  restructuring, 61
decision making, 12, 161
desk research, 62, 69, 70
difficulty, of case, 51–52, 93, 119, 121, 130
discovery, 4, 5, 7, 27, 50, 53, 85 *(see also guiding discovery)*
  process of, 16, 30
discussion, xii, 7, 11, 13, 15, 16, 17–20, 21–22, 27, 28–33, 38, 40, 43, 46, 47, 49, 50, 52, 53, 56, 84, 91, 103, 104, 107, 113, 116, 119, 121, 123, 124, 125, 127, 129, 130, 133, 134, 149, 150, 151, 159, 161, 163, 165, 166, 167, 168 *(see also awkward incident case, discussion of; Holmesafe case, discussion of)*
  closing phase, 28, 31–33, 151
  middle phase, 28, 29–31
  opening, 28–29, 30

editing, 31, 61, 84, 92, 93–100
enhancement, *see case enhancement*
examinations, 55–57, 128, 129
exercises, 111–134
exposition, 85, 119 *(see also structure, expository)*

facts and opinions, 94
feedback, 5, 6, 7, 8, 50, 53, 98, 104, 126, 129, 130, 157
field research, 62, 63–68, 69, 105

group processes, 19–20
guiding discovery, 16, 30 *(see also discovery; discovery, process of)*

Harvard, xii, 81
Holmesafe case, 21–33, 86–92, 103, 149–157
    discussion of, 21–33 *(see also awkward incident case, discussion of; discussion)*
    structure of, 86–92
    teaching note, 103, 149–157 *(see also case teaching note; teaching note)*
host organisation, 61, 64, 65–66, 67, 68, 105

incidents, 35, 36, 40, 43, 68, 165, 166, 168 *(see also case incidents)*
interpersonal skills, 19, 168 *(see also skills; teaching skills)*

knowledge, xii, 3, 4, 7, 9, 19, 21, 47, 55, 56

Lancaster model of learning, 4, 5, 6, 7, 46
learning
    objectives, 4, 15, 17, 19, 27, 45, 50, 81, 94, 101, 123, 129, 133, 138
    session, 3, 4, 8
letter requesting release of case, 105, 106, 107, 108, 109
listening, 12, 16, 65

management, xi, 21, 39, 43, 93, 95, 107, 122, 141, 142, 149, 152, 157, 161–163
McNair, Malcolm P., 81, 86, 92, 118
Midborough Technical College case, 75–80
    structure and wording of, 78–80
motivation, 28, 52, 141

narrative, 82, 100, 118 *(also see structure, narrative)*
news items, using these, 70, 113

opinions, and facts, 94
opportunities, 6, 7, 9, 27, 30, 32, 49, 50, 53, 55, 66, 85, 92, 98, 142, 150, 154 *(see also SWOT analysis)*

plot, 83, 118 *(see also structure, plot)*
polishing, 96–98, 99
preparation, 13, 63, 68, 77, 79, 137–139, 162
preparing students, 45–47
presentation, 36, 51, 52, 56, 98, 129, 155
presenting, 12, 163
pruning, 93

questions, 6, 15, 16, 17, 18, 19, 28, 30, 31, 37, 39, 50, 55, 57,
    64, 65, 66, 78, 97, 102, 103, 104, 113, 115, 116, 117, 119, 123,
    124, 129, 130, 131, 133, 134, 151
    examination, 55–57

reflection, 4, 6, 7, 27, 143
research assistant, briefing of, 68, 141–143
responses, 8, 9, 16, 29, 30, 37, 66, 151, 167
role play, 8, 41, 42
role playing, 41–43

skills, xii, 3, 4, 7, 14, 20, 43, 47, 55, 56, 65, 122 *(see also
    interpersonal skills)*
    developed by the case method, 12
    teaching, 49–53
stories, 67, 83
strengths, 27, 32, 141, 150, 154 *(see also SWOT analysis)*
structure, 8, 61, 73, 74, 78, 80, 102, 103, 109, 128, 130, 167
    (see also case structure)
    expository, 82, 85, 86, 91–92, 121, 130 *(see also exposition)*
    narrative, 82, 86–90, 121, 130 *(see also narrative)*
    plot, 82, 83, 86, 90, 121, 130 *(see also plot)*
    time, 82, 84–85, 86, 90, 121, 130 *(see also time)*
SWOT analysis, 27, 150, 154, 157 *(see also analysis;
opportunities; strengths; threats; weaknesses; written analysis)*

taking notes, during case research, 66
tasks of case teacher, 102, 159
teaching, ix, 3–10, 11, 12, 15, 16, 22, 29, 35, 36, 37, 45, 46, 49,
    50, 53, 55, 62, 63, 66, 67, 69, 70, 71, 76, 79, 81, 85, 102, 103,
    104, 105, 106, 107, 109, 113, 118, 129, 130, 138, 149, 150,
    159, 161, 163
    note, 50, 61, 100, 101, 102, 103, 104, 130 *(see also case
    teaching note; Holmesafe case, teaching note)*
    skills, 49–53
threats, 27, 32, 142, 150, 154 *(see also SWOT analysis)*
time, 65, 66, 74, 75, 82, 84, 118, 133, 142, 143, 163, 168
    (see also structure, time)
traps, for unwary case writer, 96–98

weaknesses, 27, 32, 141, 150, 154 *(see also SWOT analysis)*
written analysis, 15 *(see also analysis; SWOT analysis)*